ROUTE AND RESORTS

OF THE

CHESAPEAKE & OHIO

RAILWAY.

ILLUSTRATED.

1878

CONWAY R. HOWARD,
Gen. Pass. & Ticket Agent.

J. C. DAME,
Southern Agent.

ROUTE AND RESORTS
OF THE
CHESAPEAKE AND OHIO

RAILWAY.

ILLUSTRATED.

CONWAY R. HOWARD,
Gen. Pass. & Ticket Agent.

J. C. DAME,
Southern Agent.

Charleston, West Virginia

Charleston, West Virginia

Introduction Copyright 2023,
Quarrier Press

ISBN 13: 978-1-942294-59-7

Distributed by:

1125 Central Ave. Charleston, WV 25302
www.wvbookco.com

CONTENTS

INDEX TO ADVERTISEMENTS

Introduction to the Quarrier Press edition

On January 29, 1873, Chesapeake & Ohio (C&O) Railway officials drove a ceremonial spike at Hawks Nest, West Virginia, completing their new rail line from Richmond, Virginia, to Huntington, West Virginia. The railroad achieved George Washington's century-old dream to connect the Atlantic Ocean and Ohio River through efficient transportation. The construction lasted more than 35 years, and the arduous work—completed primarily by recently enslaved men—killed untold workers on the job while giving rise to legendary tales, such as John Henry's fabled victory over a steam-powered drill.

The C&O opened up southern West Virginia's coalfields to the world which led to an economic boom and cultural transformation summarized in two words: King Coal. It was the first railroad to cut east-west through the heart of central Appalachia and some of the most beautiful scenery in the nation.

In 1878, five years after the railroad's completion, the C&O published this travelogue of the route to promote commerce and tourism. While most people in the 19th century had little discretionary money for vacations and other frivolities, tourism would become a popular pastime for the Gilded Age's upper crust. As the authors noted in the introduction, this book was a solution to "the problem important to so many households, 'Where shall we spend the hot months of summer?'" Rather than "many households," it more accurately could have read "families with more money than they know what to do with" because most families were tending their farms just to survive, not gallivanting at expensive resorts. Much wealth still existed in the south, though, even after the Civil War had depleted much of it, and the C&O itself would make millionaires out of a few ambitious coal operators who got in early. But even for those just struggling to scrape by, railroads would become a gateway to places previously inaccessible on foot or by horse or even imagination.

The prime audience for this book were the powerful and wealthy who wanted to escape sweltering eastern cities in summer for the cool mountain air of resorts served by the C&O. For those with little or no money, these types of publications came to be known as "wish books" because they opened people's minds to a world just out of their reach. Just as George Bailey read travelogues and fantasized about traveling the world in *It's a Wonderful Life*, everyday folks in Central Appalachia had their own dreams. Publications such as this were often as far as their empty wallets could take them, but at least for a few minutes, without stepping on a train, a book like this and a little imagination could open doors to unseen places they never knew existed.

The book begins with a brief timeline of the railroad's construction, including its failed and semi-failed predecessor lines, starting with the Louisa Railroad in 1836. It brushes over the many engineering and financial letdowns, the destruction of rail lines during the Civil War that nearly ended the project, and various bankruptcies.

The tour starts in Richmond, only 13 years removed from the utter destruction left behind by the Civil War, with the Thomas Jefferson-designed capitol building of Virginia (and also that of the former Confederate States of America). Since the capitol was one of the few grand buildings in Richmond to escape the conflagration that leveled the city in 1865, much of this sight-seeing tour focuses on parks, cemeteries, and churches, including St. John's, where Patrick Henry once decried Great Britain's tyranny by declaring, "Give me liberty or give me death." The most fascinating parts focus on daily life around the Richmond wharves and warehouses, the blue-collar heart of the city that would again transform Richmond into a mid-Atlantic commercial giant.

The book then becomes a westward-heading travel guide: "From the James River Wharves, the C&O passes westerly across Bloody Run and through the Church Hill Tunnel." Each station stop on our journey includes a short history lesson. Bacon's Rebellion (1676). Redcoats under the traitor Benedict Arnold chasing the Marquis de Lafayette across the commonwealth (1781). The recent bloody clash between North and South (1861-65).

On to Hanover, Tolersville, Gordonsville, and Charlottesville, where we visit Thomas Jefferson's tomb and what he considered one of his two masterpieces: the University of Virginia. The book and all railroad life hinged on these station stops, a 19th-century ancestor of our modern interstate exits, and the small towns that blossomed wherever they were built. In this case, the C&O approximates the modern route of Interstate 64 in Virginia and U.S. Route 60 in West Virginia. As a result, the book is in many ways as relevant now as it was in the 1870s. Many interstate exits replicate the old C&O stations: Staunton, Lexington, Longdale, Lowmoor, and Clifton Forge, which would become a major railroad maintenance center and is home to the C&O Historical Society. When passengers in 1878 emerged from the pitch-dark Alleghany Tunnel, they were greeted by the sometimes-sunny state of West Virginia, which had been part of Virginia until the Civil War divided the two only 15 years before this book was published.

On to White Sulphur Springs, Lewisburg, Alderson, and the 6,400-foot Great Bend Tunnel at Talcott. While folklore identifies this as the site of John Henry's big contest, no mention is made here of the "steel-drivin' man." On to Sandstone Falls near Hinton and into the coalfields. The authors, and owners of the railroad, anticipated that the coal buried for millennia in West Virginia's mountains would fuel the United States' Industrial Revolution. Notably, the authors glossed over the inherent dangers involved with mining that coal, which would claim thousands of lives over the coming years. Instead, they promoted an implausible theory that "cheap and easy ventilation" would make accidents and explosions non-entities. On no other point is this book less accurate.

The book does, though, offer a sneak peak into the very birth of the southern West Virginia coal industry. It was one of the first to describe coal operations at places such as Quinnimont and Nuttallburg. Whitewater rafters and other tourists will recognize place names such as Fayette Station, which lies nearly directly below the New River Gorge Bridge, and picturesque wonders like Hawks Nest and Kanawha Falls.

Moving westward, the book highlights the Kanawha Valley's once-mighty salt industry—struggling to survive after the Civil War—and West Virginia's once-and-future capital city, Charleston. Our journey ends at the railroad's western terminus, Huntington, built virtually overnight from the ground up and named for C&O President Collis P. Huntington.

After completing the 421-mile train trip, the book takes a closer look at why readers should vacation on the C&O: the climate, mineral resort springs such as Old White (future site of The Greenbrier), and scenic marvels such as Natural Bridge. Even the advertisements, which comprise the last half of the book, are nostalgically absorbing, offering a sense of that period's commercial flare and reminding us of long-disappeared resorts, such as Red Sulphur Springs, West Virginia.

Perhaps most eye opening are the hand-drawn pictures throughout. Although photography was becoming more common by the late 1870s, large camera equipment and tripods were not easy to transport, and the unbearably long exposures made every good photo from this period posed in one way or another. The artists who drew these detailed pictures ranged from the famous (French painter Jules Tavernier) to the completely unknown. Thanks to their talent and attention to detail, we get rare views of railroad stations teaming with passengers, iron ore and coal mining, skilled boatsmen running the New River Gorge's treacherous rapids on nothing but log rafts, timber drives down the Greenbrier River, the Kanawha Valley saltworks, and some of the best early views of Charleston and Huntington, burgeoning towns that would soon become West Virginia's largest.

So, get ready to time-travel and catch a glimpse of life in central Virginia and West Virginia nearly 150 years ago. Imagine the beautiful sights all around you and of being a part of the history being made in 1878. How does the scenery look without the sounds of interstates, car horns, and the other cacophonies of modern times? As you flip from page to page, gaze out your own window. Bet you can almost hear the steam whistle and clickety-clack of train wheels taking you back to another time and to places beyond your own imaginations.

Stan Bumgardner, 2023

ROUTE AND RESORTS
OF THE CHESAPEAKE & OHIO RAILWAY.

VIEW ON THE GREENBRIER.

INTRODUCTORY.

The purpose of the following pages is to give a condensed sketch of the Chesapeake and Ohio Railway, "when and how built," and the more interesting localities upon its line; also important information to the tourist, invalid and pleasure-seeker concerning its various and famous mineral springs and summer resorts, and how to reach them; and, in short, to aid in the solution of the problem, important to so many households, "Where shall we spend the hot months of summer?"

It is also intended to notice briefly, in passing, the character of the magnificent country rendered accessible by this railroad; its development, and industrial improvements; its advantages for residence and the opportunity presented to settlers for desirable homes at moderate cost, in a healthy region, which, from its peculiar climate and gradual rise from the sea coast, permits the cultivation of nearly every important crop known in the United States.

CHESAPEAKE & OHIO RAILWAY.

I.

WHEN AND HOW BUILT.

The line of railway, completed and operated under the Chesapeake and Ohio organization, was built to connect the Western systems of transportation with those of the Atlantic Seaboard; and with foreign commerce, by the Chesapeake Bay and its affluents. Richmond, Va., and Huntington, W. Va., distant 421 miles, by rail, are its terminal cities.

As with all the great trunk lines of the United States, its beginning was small—for local uses and under the "Louisa Railroad" Charter. But even then the idea existed of future extension to the Ohio River, which steadily grew in the public mind as the State surveys brought into prominent notice the very valuable mineral deposits of the mountain districts now traversed by the Chesapeake and Ohio Railroad. And more important, as men then thought, was the determination (by the same surveys) of the engineering fact, that the Alleghany mountains could be crossed in Central Virginia at a lower elevation and with more favorable gradients than had previously been deemed practicable in first-class railroad construction.

Thus the State of Virginia became interested in the enterprise—directly, by undertaking the construction of the Blue Ridge and the Covington and Ohio Railroads, and indirectly by State subscription, under the general law, to the "Virginia Central Railroad Company," into which the old Louisa Railroad was merged in 1850.

It may be of interest to recall in this connection a few leading facts and dates now rapidly passing from public memory.

Ground was first broken on the Louisa Railroad in October, 1836. Track was completed to Frederick's Hall in 1838; to Louisa Court-House in 1839, and to Gordonsville in 1840. Here the extension rested until 1847, when work was resumed, and in 1848 the track reached Cobham; in 1850 the Rivanna River; and in December, 1852, Mechum's River, the eastern terminus of the Blue Ridge Railroad—commenced under the legislative enactment of 1849, to tunnel the Blue Ridge mountain and to connect again with the Virginia Central Railroad on the south fork of the Shenandoah River at Waynesboro'.

The Blue Ridge tunnel, prosecuted under many difficulties, was finally opened to travel in April, 1858. But in advance, the Virginia Central Railroad Company in 1853-'4 constructed a temporary track over the mountain, (and through the Rock Fish Gap,) connecting at Waynesboro' with its main track partially completed to Staunton. This mountain track (with maximum grades of 295 6-10 feet per mile) attracted much attention at the time from its successful operation and the substantial value of the results accomplished.

In 1854 trains ran to Staunton; in 1855 to Goshen; in 1856 to Millboro,' and in July, 1857, to Jackson's River Station, 195 miles from Richmond. It may be noted that a second temporary track (300 feet per mile, maximum grade) was used around the unfinished Lick Run embankment, two miles west of Millboro', and with the same success as the Blue Ridge incline, until the completion of the permanent embankment.

The track rested at Jackson's River during the political troubles, and until 1867-'8, when means were provided to complete the remaining ten miles to Covington, the eastern terminus of the Covington and Ohio Railroad, and 205 miles from Richmond.

That work was commenced by the State of Virginia, to connect the Virginia Central Railroad and the projected James River and Kanawha Canal with the Kentucky Railroad system near the confluence of the Big Sandy and Ohio rivers. The location called for a maximum grade of 30 feet per mile from the Ohio River, over the Alleghany mountain divide, to the Jackson's Fork of James River and Covington, and in the reverse direction (of lighter traffic) a maximum of 60 feet per mile to ascend the eastern slope of the Alleghany mountain.

These very low grades necessitated a much bolder and more costly character of graduation and masonry than had previously been deemed admissable in American railroad construction; and this being regarded beyond the ability of private or corporate capital, was undertaken by the State, under the direction of its Board of Public Works. Yet, eventually, it was reserved for an association of individual capitalists to complete this great improvement.

Work was commenced under the Covington and Ohio organization in 1855, and so progressed until the general suspension of 1861, up to which date a large amount of graduation and masonry of excellent execution had been done upon the mountain division, and to some, but much less extent further west, between the Kanawha and Big Sandy rivers.

After the war it was found impracticable to continue this construction as a State work; and in 1868 an entire reörganization was effected, under enactments of the Virginia and West Virginia legislatures, consolidating into the Chesapeake and Ohio Railroad Company all of the previous organizations, or divisions, of the line, from Richmond to the Ohio River; and ceding to the new company, under certain conditions, the State property in the Blue Ridge and the Covington and Ohio railroads.

The Chesapeake and Ohio Railroad Company then proceeded to complete the mountain division (with the use of temporary tracks around, or over, two tunnels and at the unfinished Jerry's Run embankment)—sufficiently to open travel to the White Sulphur Springs, 227 miles from Richmond, in July, 1869.

From the White Sulphur Springs to Huntington there now remained 194 miles of difficult construction, comprising the longest tunnel and the heaviest bridging of the line, through a country then unusually inaccessible and deficient in supplies; and the prices of railroad labor and materials were at their maximum.

The work was promptly undertaken by the new company and was pressed with vigor over all obstacles until January, 1873, when the entire line of track from Richmond to Huntington was successfully connected.* During the same time, the large amount of unfinished work on the mountain grades between Millboro' and the White Sulphur was prosecuted to completion.

All of this construction was of very superior quality—double track masonry west of Covington, iron bridge superstructure of the best design, steel rails in large proportion, large and well-built machine shops and depot buildings, and an excellent general equipment. The road-bed and structures between Covington and Richmond have also been much improved; and the Chesapeake and Ohio Railroad, as completed, is one of the most solidly constructed, as it has proved to be one of the safest lines in the country.

American railway annals are not wanting in striking examples of persistent purpose, splendid energy, and financial skill and achievment. Among such examples, in a period remarkable for great public improvements, the construction of the Chesapeake and Ohio Railroad, is not the least notable.

---

* The first spike of the Louisa Railroad and the last of the C. & O. track connection was driven by C. R. Mason, the first superintendent of the former, and since largely engaged in the construction of the latter, and in mining enterprises on its line.

II.

DESCRIPTIVE.

The Chesapeake and Ohio Railroad, from its varied and beautiful scenery and the many localities of interest—historic, mineral and commercial—upon its line, has become a favorite route for the tourist. It is especially frequented by that large class of travellers who annually seek the Virginia mountains and springs for health and pleasure.

To meet inquiries frequently addressed to officers of the railroad, the following brief sketch has been prepared of the line and its more prominent localities.

RICHMOND.

This city, the capital of Virginia, distant 74 miles, air-line, from ocean navigation at the entrance of Hampton Roads, is built at and around the Falls of James River.

The first recorded English settlement, as given in the "Historical Collections of Virginia," was in 1609, or eleven years before the landing at Plymouth Rock. In 1644-'5, after the Indian disasters of the colony, its "fforte Charles" was erected; in 1737 it was laid off, and in 1742 established "by law, as a town;" and in 1779 Richmond became the seat of government, after the removal from Williamsburg, during the war of the revolution. Its subsequent history is too prominently connected with that of the entire country to require further mention.

The site of Richmond has been often noticed in books for the picturesque beauty of its river scenery and surroundings. Very attractive views of James River and the Falls may be had from Church and Gamble's Hills, and from Hollywood and other elevated points which have been left along the front of the original bluff or plateau, now so deeply worn into valleys and hollows by its present lines of drainage.

Topographically, the city is divided into two principal sections, viz.: the lower and older, located with reference to commerce and manufactures; and the upper, for residence and suburban extension.

The climate of Richmond is indicated in the annual table of temperature elsewhere given. It is above the line of malaria of the lower country, and below the winter rigor of the mountains beyond. Northern visitors, on their way to the far South, constantly linger in Richmond, and many remain during the colder months.

The growth of Richmond will appear from the following census returns of its population for the past sixty years:

In 1820,	-	-	-	-	6,974
" 1830,	-	-	-	-	16,060
" 1840,	-	-	-	-	20,153
" 1850,	-	-	-	-	27,570
" 1860,	-	-	-	-	37,907
" 1870,	-	-	-	-	51,038

And in 1878 the population of Richmond (resident and floating) is estimated at 77,500 by the Board of Health and other city officials charged with its general administration.

PUBLIC BUILDINGS AND GROUNDS.

The State "Capitol," from its commanding site and very attractive grounds, is particularly conspicuous. It was designed after a celebrated Roman structure (the *Maison Carre* of Nismes), and was completed in 1792. If not impressive for architectural completeness, it is still so rich in historic associations and relics, and interesting in connection with the State Library and statuary, as to be much visited by strangers.

Outside of the Capitol the Washington, the Stonewall-Jackson and the Clay Monuments will repay careful examination. Several of the statues which adorn them are considered by connoisseurs to have high artistic merit.

Among other leading places of interest to visitors may be mentioned the Monroe Square in the upper district of the city; the Marshall and (projected) Chimborazo parks, and the Oakwood and National cemeteries in the lower district; the old Reservoir, with the attractive cemetery grounds of Hollywood adjoining; the new Reservoir beyond, with its broad avenues and promising City Park; the old Monumental Church, associated with the Richmond Theatre catas-

THE TREDEGAR IRON WORKS—RICHMOND.

trophe upon its site in 1811; the venerable St. John's Church of Church Hill, with which history connects the most eloquent utterances of Patrick Henry before the revolutionary war, and other churches memorable for local associations; the Richmond and Medical Colleges and the Public Schools; the large flour mills, Haxall, Gallego and Manchester, so long identified with the commercial prosperity of Richmond; the Tredegar, Old Dominion, and other iron and machine works equally identified with the material development of the city; the Tobacco Exchange, the City Water and Gas Works, the many bridges, railroad, and highway over James River, the canal ship dock and locks, and the railroad tunnels as works of engineering note; and for architects and all concerned in the building art, the quarries on either bank of James River which supply the beautiful granite now so widely used for choice monumental and building stone, and as a preferred paving material for first-class streets. The Richmond Custom House and Postoffice, the stone work of the Monuments in the Capitol Square, the United States State Department in Washington and Postoffice in Philadelphia present fine examples of this granite.

GALLEGO MILLS—RICHMOND.

RICHMOND COMMERCE

is steadily recovering from the effect of its nearly total suspension from 1861 to 1865. During the year 1877 the Harbor Master reported the arrival of 903 sailing vessels and 570 steamers, with a total tonnage of 677,000 tons, being about 25 per ct. increase over 1876.

This aggregate includes 131,516 barrels of flour for Brazil—a slight increase over the shipments of 1876; but the larger increase comes from the business of the Chesapeake and Ohio Railroad. From the James River wharves of this Company, which are provided with superior facilities for transhipment, 546 sailing vessels were loaded during 1877—against 477 in 1876—with coals, oil, timber, grain, cotton, copper and manganese, and general merchandise for eastern and European ports.

Regular lines of steamers ply between Richmond and the cities of New York, Philadelphia, Baltimore and Norfolk.

MANUFACTURES.

The fine water power of the James River Falls marks Richmond as a place of manufacturing importance. The elevation of the first level of the James River and Kanawha Canal is 81 feet above mean tide in, or below, its ship lock. At several points below the level of this feeder, and along the rapids, an abundant water supply is drawn off for the City Water Works, and many manufac-

EARTH-WORKS ON THE CHICKAHOMINY, NEAR RICHMOND.

turing establishments upon both banks of the river—including all the large flouring mills, the Tredegar Iron Works, the Old Dominion Nail Works, the Franklin Paper Mills, Marshall and Old Dominion Cotton Mills and others. In addition to those operated by water-power, there are several iron works and foundries—the Metropolitan, Talbott, Ettenger & Edmund, and the Richmond Foundry—which use steam-power to advantage, from the low cost of the Chesapeake and Ohio, and other coals.

Among the more important industries of Richmond, the Tobacco Manufacture appears to be of special interest to strangers, who seldom omit to visit the warehouses and factories. In December, 1877, there were 79 separate establishments in operation connected with this trade, and which employed 5,868 hands.

The annual Trade Review, (*Dispatch* Jan. 1, 1878,) after referring to the depression in the tobacco and iron markets, adds: "Many of our manufactures show a largely improved business, notably in agricultural implements, bricks, and other builders' materials, leather goods, cigars, clothing, cotton goods, flour, fertilizers, and all kinds of small wares, while nearly one thousand more hands have been employed than in 1876."

The sales of the products of the Richmond manufacturers during 1877, amounted to $21,966,397.

LEAVING RICHMOND.

From the James River Wharves, the Chesapeake and Ohio Railroad passes westerly across Bloody Run and through the Church Hill Tunnel (3,927 feet in length) into the valley of Shockoe creek, where are located the company's offices, depot buildings, shops and the distributing coal bins for the Richmond city trade.

Thence ascending the slopes of Shockoe creek, the line cuts through the low dividing ridge, and descending to the Chickahominy bottoms, crosses that river about six miles from the Richmond depot, and where it is little more than creek-wide.

All this ground is of historical interest. Bloody Run was the scene of the fight of 1656, in which the Rangers, under Col. Edward Hill, and the friendly Indians, under Totopotomoi (the Pamunkey chief), were defeated, and the latter slain, by a large force of "Ricaherian Indians from the mountains."

Gillie's creek, Shockoe creek and its Bacon's Quarter branch are associated with important events in the early history of the "Bacon Rebellion" of 1676; and afterwards, in 1781, with the engagement of the State militia against the British expeditionary forces under Arnold and Simcoe.

More recently, from 1862 to 1864, the Chesapeake and Ohio crossing of the Chickahominy defined the boundary of the field

WICKHAM'S STATION.

GORDONSVILLE—LOCAL COMMISSARY DEPARTMENT.

of combat around Richmond from 1862 to 1865. Field-works still remain to mark the lines of strife, now happily of more interest to the military student than to all others.

ATLEE'S STATION,

nine miles from Richmond depot, Totopotomoi creek and all the country on to Hanover Junction, is notable in the same connection; and also for military movements of Lafayette in 1781, whose line of retrograde march to a junction with Wayne, at Raccoon Ford of the Rapidan, passed not far to the eastward—a retreat which was soon to become an advance halting at Yorktown.

Reverting to the "plough-share"—it is well known that the agricultural system of Virginia experienced violent changes after 1865, and mainly from the changed conditions of labor. How well and wisely these changes have been met can be no where better seen than from the car-windows of the

Chesapeake and Ohio Railroad in passing the Chickahominy bottoms, going up through the smaller ridge or upland farms to Hanover Court-House; and beyond, over the larger farms around the upper-waters of the Pamunkey River and its branches, the North and South Anna. No section of Virginia exhibits more substantial recuperation.

This successful culture of the light soils of Hanover county suggests allusion to the marl (calcareous earth) of Eastern Virginia, which, cheaply excavated, forms a good fertilizer, either alone or judiciously used in combination.

HANOVER COUNTY,

in Colonial times, was of much greater territorial extent than at present. Then, tobacco was the leading crop, and some 1,600 hogsheads were annually exported from Hanover Town, 10 miles down the Pamunkey River from the Chesapeake and Ohio Railroad, near Hanover Court-House. Now, the more important products are wheat, corn and fruit; and the melon crop is one of the most remunerative.

HANOVER COURT-HOUSE,

eighteen and one-fourth miles from Richmond, is associated with many historical incidents and names. Patrick Henry and Henry Clay were born in its vicinity; and the old Court-House building, constructed in 1735 with imported brick, is memorable for its colonial and revolutionary reminiscences.

AT HANOVER JUNCTION,

26 miles from Richmond, the Chesapeake and Ohio Railroad crosses the Richmond, Fredericksburg and Potomac Railroad, and, turning westerly, follows the ridge dividing the water shed of the North and the South Anna rivers. The ridge country, immediately upon the line of the railroad, hardly indicates the better soil on the slopes and in the bottoms on either side, which supply the local business for the frequent depots along this division.

AT TOLERSVILLE STATION

there are abundant evidences of the mining operations of the vicinity, noted elsewhere.

FREDERICK'S HALL,

with its tobacco factory, indicates the special crop of the vicinity—a very high grade of the finer tobaccos.

LOUISA COURT-HOUSE, 62 miles from Richmond, was formerly the terminus of the Louisa Railroad. It is the market town of a considerable agricultural district, and contributes materially to the traffic of the railroad.

TREVILIAN'S STATION was an important point of battle in the cavalry operations of 1864, and is the railroad outlet of the fertile Green Springs district. Not far to the Southwest is the military road cut by Lafayette in pursuit of the

English forces in 1781, and which still bears the name of the "Marquis Road."

GORDONSVILLE,

in Orange county, marks the intersection of the Chesapeake and Ohio and the Virginia Midland railroads; and is a dining station for both. Thence, to Charlottesville the Virginia Midland uses the Chesapeake and Ohio track.

Five miles west of Gordonsville the line descends towards the Rivanna River on the slopes of Matchunk creek, skirting the foothills of Peter's (Southwest) mountain, and traversing one of the richest agricultural belts of Virginia—the celebrated "chocolate" lands of Orange and Albemarle counties.

COBHAM STATION,

in the fairest section of this valley, is within distant sight of the church of the "Blind Preacher," rendered memorable by the touching sketch of William Wirt. The old structure has given place to a beautiful and enduring edifice, built through the efforts and liberality of the honored lady of the adjoining estate.

SHADWELL STATION,

ninety-three miles from Richmond, and on

JEFFERSON'S OLD MILL—SHADWELL.

UNIVERSITY OF VIRGINIA.

the Rivanna River, was the old mill property of Thomas Jefferson: the ruins still remain.

Two miles on, the Chesapeake and Ohio Railroad, crossing the Rivanna, passes through the "water gap" of the Southwest mountain. On the south bank, overlooking the railroad-track, is Monticello ("Little Mountain,") the famed retreat of the celebrated statesman, and also remembered for its magnificent view of the Piedmont country and its superb Blue Ridge background. Not far on, and 97 miles from

JEFFERSON'S TOMB

Richmond, the railroad reaches Charlottesville, the county seat of Albemarle county, and where, in 1781, the legislature met after the occupation of lower Virginia, and again dispersed after the rapid cavalry advance of Tarleton to this place in 1781.

Charlottesville is the railroad center of one of the most productive and locally attractive districts of the entire Southern country. The surrounding vineyards, orchards (with their Albemarle pippin,) gardens and farms, rivalling the best in fertility and culture, well attest what has been said and written of this favored locality. Its woollen mills, foundry, manufactory of agricultural implements and many other industries, are further suggestive of the wants and resources of the vicinity.

It is the point of divergence of the Virginia Midland Railroad and of transfer for passengers to the Southwest. Above the angle of intersection of the two railroads, and just beyond the Charlottesville town-limits, is the University of Virginia.

This noted institution of learning was founded by Thomas Jefferson, under a legislative enactment of 1817-'8, and was in full operation in 1825. Liberally endowed by the State, it has taken a high position among its compeers from the requirements of its course, the personal attainments of many eminent members of its faculty, and the distinguished public men enumerated in its list of graduates. It is steadily recovering its ante-bellum prestige, and has again become, with its beautiful surroundings, its halls, arcades, scientific appliances, paintings and cabinets, a place of more than ordinary interest to the educated visitor.

The more recent structures, the Chemical Laboratory and the handsome Museum Building, with its instructive and growing collections, (built through the liberality of a donor, whose name was withheld during his life, Mr. Brooks, of Rochester, N. Y.,) are valuable additions to what have preceded. The accompanying illustration gives an excellent bird's-eye-view of the University of Virginia.

From Charlottesville to Mechum's River there lies a fine rolling country, presenting many attractive sites for the better class of country residences, or villas. Crossing Mechum's River at an elevation of 550 feet above tide-level, the Chesapeake and Ohio Railroad commences the ascent of the Blue Ridge.

This mountain range, so widely known through 'Jefferson's Notes on Virginia,' first takes its distinctive name at Harper's Ferry on the Potomac, and retains it through Virginia, the Carolinas and Georgia. As far south as the vicinity of Christiansburg, Va., it is an outlying or flank range of the Alleghany chain, with an average elevation of 2,500 to 3,500 feet above sea-level—with spurs or peaks occasionally higher and with frequent depressions or gaps. It is penetrated by the James River, which heads against the Alleghany Mountain proper; but south of the James, the Blue Ridge rises in elevation (in Northern Georgia over 5,000 feet above tide), and becomes the true divide between the Atlantic and Mississippi waters.

The Chesapeake and Ohio Railroad passes this mountain barrier with an average gradient of 70 per mile, equated for curves and straight line. The graduation is heavy; with much rock excavation, three spur tunnels, and the main tunnel, 4,260 feet in length, under the Ridge Summit. At the date of its construction this tunnel was one of the longest in the United States, and having been driven without shafts, it was the subject of much notice in public and professional circles.

One of the most beautiful panoramic views, or succession of views, on the line of this railroad, is presented in the Blue Ridge ascent. The upper valleys of the Rock Fish River and its branches are spread out far below, enclosed on the left by the Southwest range of hills, and opposite by the more elevated Blue Ridge—with a very pleasing contrast of wild and cultivated ground, of farms, groves and vineyards opposed by rocks, ravines and the roughest aspects of mountain scenery. Nature is seldom seen more picturesque, or human art in bolder undertaking, close by.

The high Blue Ridge peak to the southward, before entering the tunnel, is the "Pinnacle" mountain—a principal signal station of the Coast Survey Triangulation.

GREENWOOD AND AFTON

are the two railroad stations on this grade, and on the ridge above is Mountain Top—all pleasant summer retreats.

The railroad passes through the Blue Ridge tunnel at an elevation of 1,500 feet above tide-level, and descends into the Valley of Virginia, crossing the South Fork of the Shenandoah River 1,284 feet above tide. Thence the railroad crosses the Valley transversely, and 20 miles on ascends the slopes

STAUNTON—VIEW FROM THE RAILROAD.

BUFFALO GAP AND FURNACE.

of its western rim—the North Mountain.

WAYNESBORO' STATION

is the point of shipment for the manganese mines of Turk's Mountain, the Virginia (Mt. Torry) Iron Furnace, and of the Kaolin Works when in operation. Its flour and plaster mills and local manufactures supply the wants of a rich farming district.

FISHERSVILLE STATION,

5 miles beyond, is the railroad outlet for another section of this fine valley country. Its Lime Quarries and Kilns ship an excellent lime both east and west.

STAUNTON,

the next station, and 136 miles from Richmond, is the county seat of Augusta county, and one of the most flourishing towns of the Valley of Virginia. From its elevated situation, healthy climate, and beautiful mountain views, this city was selected by the State for the site of its asylums for the Blind, the Insane, and the Deaf and Dumb.

There are also located in Staunton the seminaries of several leading religious denominations, viz.: the "Augusta Female Seminary," Presbyterian; the "Virginia Female Institute," Episcopalian; the "Wesleyan Female Institute," Methodist; and the "Staunton Female Seminary," Lutheran. These institutions have been long noted for good management and educational success.

They have a large attendance, and contribute much to the attractiveness of the place.

Staunton is the junction of the Chesapeake and Ohio and the Valley Railroads (the latter giving access to Weyer's Cave and other localities of interest down to Harper's Ferry), and the distributing point of a large area of the Valley country. The Augusta or Stribling Springs are twelve miles distant from the Chesapeake and Ohio Railroad by stage road.

The population of Staunton is estimated to exceed 6,500, and steadily increases. There are local gas and water works, and all the mechanical industries of a busy, enterprising inland city.

Passing the Chesapeake and Ohio engine-houses, near the western corporate limits, the line of road pursues a generally direct course toward the Buffalo Gap of the Little North Mountain, through which it continues to ascend to North Mountain station, 150 miles from Richmond, and

VIEW OF IRON ORE MINES, FERROL FURNACE, VA.

2,070 feet above tide-level, which is the highest grade elevation of the entire line. Immediately to the northward of this summit gap rises "Elliot's Knob," (the Great North Mountain) to a height of 4,480 feet above the sea: it is another signal station of the United States Coast Survey.

In the Buffalo Gap are two furnaces of the Virginia Iron and Steel Company.

THE VARIETY SPRINGS,

five miles beyond, are in full view of Elliot's Knob, and the Little Calf-pasture Valley at its base.

WASHINGTON-LEE UNIVERSITY—LEXINGTON, VA.

AT ELIZABETH STATION,

the Ferrol Iron Furnace (Call and Jones) has been repaired, enlarged and put in blast. The local ores, from the immense hematite deposits of the vicinity, are here used successfully, with the New River coke for fuel. This, and the adjoining property, (the Estiline,) are among the oldest and best known of the Virginia furnace tracts.

POND GAP

is the station for Crawford Springs, one mile distant from the railroad; and also on the lower slopes of Elliot's Knob.

CRAIGSVILLE STATION

is the point of shipment for the marble quarries near by, which supply ornamental stone of fine color and quality; and in demand at Cincinnati and other distant cities.

BELL'S VALLEY STATION

is the outlet of the "Wilson and Preston" ore deposits—a continuation on the North Mountain slopes, of the Elizabeth and Estiline.

GOSHEN STATION,

168 miles from Richmond, is the stage station for Lexington, (20 miles distant,) the Rockbridge Baths, (9 miles,) the Rockbridge and Jordan Alum Springs, (9 miles,) the Cold Sulphur, (2 miles,) and of the well-known furnace properties of the vicinity (the Lydia, Gay's Run, New Hope, California, Australia and others) of considerable local importance in the past, and now owned chiefly by Pennsylvania iron-masters.

The road from Goshen to the Rockbridge Baths and Lexington, passes through the North River Gap—one of the most picturesque routes in the Virginia mountains.

LEXINGTON,

as an educational centre, and

THE VIRGINIA MILITARY INSTITUTE—LEXINGTON, VA.

GRIFFITH'S KNOB AND COW PASTURE RIVER.

from its vicinity to the Natural Bridge and other interesting localities, is much visited. The Washington-Lee University, founded by Gen. Washington, and afterwards presided over by Gen. Lee, continues its excellent course of instruction, with an able staff of professors and the necessary apparatus and library facilities for an institution of its grade. The Virginia Military Institute, on the adjoining grounds, sustains its high reputation as the first military school of the Southern States. A very fine mountain view is presented from the elevated plateau upon which both institutions are located. Lexington possesses peculiar interest for many travellers, from its historic associations and as the resting place of Generals Lee and Stonewall Jackson.

Returning to the Chesapeake and Ohio Railroad, the tourist will be struck with the wild scenery of the Panther Gap gorge, the point of passage through the Mill Mountain. A small iron furnace beyond has been built to work the local ores; also a deposit of manganese has been opened in the vicinity for

shipment to the Bromine Works westward.

MILLBORO' STATION,

on the high ridge beyond, is a point of departure for the Rockbridge Alum Springs, 6 miles, and the Jordan Alum, 5 miles, distant to the southward; and in the opposite direction, the Millboro', 2 miles, and the Wallawhatoola, 3 miles, the Bath Alum, 10 miles, the Warm, 15 miles, the Healing, 23 miles, and the Hot, 20 miles. The medicinal qualities of these celebrated springs are referred to elsewhere. There are good hotel accommodations at Millboro' for travellers, and especially invalids *en route;* and the drive thence to any of the springs named is pleasantly remembered for the beautiful mountain views and scenery in all directions.

Descending from the Millboro' ridge to the Cow-pasture and Jackson's Forks of James River, the line of road passes through several tunnels and over a series of heavy embankments, one of which is 160 feet fill—a bold location through a difficult country. The most prominent topographical feature is the Griffith Knob, the abrupt termination of Rough Mountain on the Cow-pasture, and a noted land mark of surveyors. Its sharp outline, in a sandstone and shale formation, arrests attention.

LONGDALE STATION

and Peter's Switch are points of shipment for the Longdale Iron Company, (Firmstone, Pardee & Co.,) which operate (seven miles distant by their branch track) a successful iron furnace, supplied with coke from the company's mines at Sewell station on New River, 130 miles westward. The working results of the Longdale Furnace are regarded with much interest by iron-masters, both from the small percentage of fuel (coke) used in reducing the local ores, and the excellent quality of the iron made. The furnace product is shipped chiefly westward, to Cincinnati and other points of the Ohio River.

PARTIAL VIEW OF CLIFTON FORGE WATER-GAP AND NATURAL ARCH.

CLIFTON FORGE STATION,

191 miles from Richmond, and 1,047 feet above tide-level, is directly opposite a remarkable water-gap cut through a spur, or prolongation of Waite's Mountain, and through which pass the waters of the Jackson Fork of James River and its numerous tributaries. The area of this mountain drainage is very nearly one thousand square miles, extending from the Potomac watershed northeast, in Highland county, to that of the Ohio in the vicinity of the Salt Pond, of Giles county, to the southwest; and laterally from the Alleghany divide to the Cow-pasture Mountain, and other flank ranges eastward. The discharge of this considerable basin has, in time, worn through the mountain barrier at Clifton Forge, breaking down a precipitous gorge, only 250 feet wide at its base, and with bold, high cliffs on either side, nearly perpendicular. Through this natural pass have been constructed the James River and Kanawha turnpike, and the Clifton Forge and Buchanan Railroad—the latter still incomplete. The James River and Kanawha canal location also used this gate-way, of ample dimensions to pass all.

Apart from other attractions, the locality is of peculiar geological interest. Whatever force cut, or created, the gorge, also laid bare one of the finest anti-clinal sections of American geology. The sand-stone ledges (Rogers N^3) of the mountain have been uplifted, preserving lines of singular symmetry, and in two regular defined segmental niches —the upper, 2,500 feet chord and 438 feet rise; and the lower 1,250 feet chord by 240 feet rise. Between these sand-stone ledges,

and concentric with the upper, lies a valuable seam of fossiliferous iron ore, which is mined for the Quinnimont Furnace of West Virginia, 103 miles westward.

The distant mountain range, seen from the cars as the back ground of the beautiful view through the Clifton Forge Gap, is the Richpatch, a South-western extension of the Mill Mountain group—all noted for their rich deposits of iron ores. Mineral springs are frequent in the vicinity: one mile from the old forge the Keyser's Springs, and ten miles the Dagger's Springs, with accommodations for visitors.

Three and a half miles from the railroad station is the Callie Iron Furnace; and along the James River Valley, below, several of the more noted furnace properties of old repute.

WILLIAMSON'S STATION,

one mile beyond Clifton Forge, is one of the most important coaling stations of the Chesapeake and Ohio engine service.

JACKSON'S RIVER STATION

was, for several years, the terminus of the Virginia Central, before it passed into the Chesapeake and Ohio Railroad. The high grounds north of Jackson's River are the slopes and foot-hills of the Warm Spring Mountain, and of the most elevated of the Alleghany parallel ranges.

LOWMOOR STATION

is the junction of the branch track (2¾ miles) from the Lowmoor Iron Ore Mines, which supply the Quinnimont Furnace and ship hematite ores to several Ohio River furnaces between Wheeling and Cincinnati.

ALLEGHANY TUNNEL.

The Lowmoor ores are chiefly hematite and fossiliferous. but embrace the "block" and all the iron ores of this well-known belt. They make a strong foundry and mill iron, which is in demand along the Ohio Valley, from Pittsburg to St. Louis, and eastward to Richmond and Baltimore; and they run over 50 per cent. in the furnace. These mines have been extensively opened, and present an ore section of over 100 feet vertical depth by 30 feet or more transverse thickness in a single seam—with other seams but partially opened—in every respect one of the most interesting ore exposures of the entire mineral district. The finer Lowmoor ores are passed through washers worked with steam power, and are otherwise unusually well prepared for distant transportation.

A large iron furnace has been planned, and before long is to be built on the furnace property of the Lowmoor Co., near the railroad.

AT STEELE'S STATION—

and on either side of the river— to the southward on the Richpatch Mountain and along its north- ward spurs, and across the river on the lower slopes of the Warm

2

Spring Mountain—including the "Dolly Ann" Furnace property—these valuable hem- atite deposits continue through a district destined to be one of the largest iron pro- ducing belts of the United States.

COVINGTON,

the Fort Young, or Covington, of Indian times, and the county seat of Alleghany county, (205 miles by railroad from Rich- mond and 1,245 feet above tide,) has before been mentioned as the eastern terminus of the old Covington and Ohio railroad, as projected, and afterwards consolidated into the Chesapeake and Ohio. It is also the stage station for the Healing Springs, 15 miles distant; the Hot, 18 miles, and the Warm, 23 miles. The road to these springs is of the very pleasing character marking nearly all in this beautiful mountain region; and one of the most attractive features of the drive is the well-known "Falling Springs."

Covington, at the eastern foot of the Alle- ghany foot-hills, may be considered the com- mencement of the ascending grades of the great water divide between the Atlantic and the Mississippi. The passage of this mountain barrier is described in the following spirited

JERRY'S RUN.

sketch from the "Tourist Edition of Batchelder's Popular Resorts:"

"After crossing Jackson's River a third time, the road follows the valley of Dunlap's creek for five miles, crossing the creek four times with bridges of a hundred and thirty feet opening, and makes two tunnels and several very heavy cuttings. It then ascends by a grade of sixty feet per mile a rugged mountain slope, with excavations and embankments following each other in rapid succession, unequalled, it is believed, in this or any other country. There are a great number of cuts of sixty feet in depth, many over a hundred, and the slopes of some reach even to a hundred and fifty feet above grade. Each of these interesting results of engineering skill adds new and fresh artistic features for the tourist's gratification. The embankments are equal in magnitude. That over "Moss Run" is a hundred and forty feet in depth; over Jerry's Run a hundred and eighty-five feet. The lower slope stakes of the latter were over two hundred feet below grade. These streams cross the road by tunnels cut in the rocky sides of the ravines, tunnels ample in size to pass a railroad train. The embankment at Jerry's Run contains over a million cubic yards of material. It is on a gentle curve, which is produced on either side for some distance, and views of it can be had from several points on the road; but even this huge mass is dwarfed by the mighty hills which surround it, so insignificant are the works of man when brought face to face with those of nature. After crossing the great embankment, the road follows a ravine, and in a short time enters Lewis Tunnel. This is about four thousand feet long, and is cut through hard rock, through a spur called the Little Alleghany, and, including its approaches, is seven thousand feet from grade to grade. It was worked from two shafts as well as from the ends, and is a continuous grade of sixty feet per mile. After passing this tunnel the road encounters the main Alleghany, which is pierced with a tunnel nearly forty-eight hundred feet in length, passing four hundred and fifty-eight feet below its crest. The Summit level is on the eastern side, 2,060 feet above tide, and from its ditches the water flows at will, either to the Atlantic or the Gulf of Mexico. The grade descends through the tunnel at the rate of thirty feet per mile; and the road, now on the affluents of the Kanawha, descends with the streams, losing nothing by undulations, the grade nowhere exceeding thirty feet per mile; and after clearing the Alleghany, twelve miles west of the tunnel, with nothing over twenty feet per mile until steamboat navigation is reached (until sixteen miles below Charleston, in fact) a distance of a hundred and sixty miles, with gentle curvature, forming one of the grandest and best constructed roads between the East and the West."

ALLEGHANY STATION,

222 miles from Richmond, at the eastern portal of the Alleghany Tunnel, is the stage station of the Old Sweet Springs, of pleasant celebrity, nine miles distant; and of the Red, or Sweet Chalybeate, adjoining.

RAFTING ON GREENBRIER RIVER.

SECOND CREEK TUNNEL DURING CONSTRUCTION.

The White Sulphur Springs are more fully described in the sketch of the Virginia watering places, further on; but the passenger, from the car-windows, will not fail to notice the beautiful valleys, the bold scenery and many choice sites for villas—which, when the suspense of court-action (that has so long clouded this fair domain) comes to a termination, will be sought as one of the most charming of American mountain retreats; and like Newport, for permanent residence.

CALDWELL'S STATION,

1,765 feet above tide-level, marks another interesting water-gap, through which Howard's creek and its tributaries unite with the Greenbrier River. The railroad line tunnels the steep mountain, locally known as the White Rock, and also one of the prolongations of the Greenbrier range. Beyond the mouth of Howard's creek opens out the Greenbrier Valley, a rich limestone belt parallel with the Shenandoah Valley eastward, and some 450 feet higher on the railroad profile, but rising much more rapidly towards the Greenbrier headwaters.

LEWISBURG,

the county seat of Greenbrier county, is nearly equi-distant from Caldwell and Ronceverte stations, and about four miles off. It is a place of note in the history of this country—

The stage road descends to Dunlap's creek at the old "Crow" tavern, famous in the past, and thence passes up the Creek Valley to the springs (which are appropriately noticed elsewhere), and in full view of the Beaver Dam Falls, a pretty little cascade also interesting from the calcareous tufa deposits of the vicinity.

WHITE SULPHUR STATION,

five miles beyond Alleghany and 1,920 feet above the sea, is immediately at the entrance of that delightful and widely know watering place, so often styled the Saratoga of the South. The spring grounds are located in a lovely mountain cove on the lower slopes of Kate's Mountain, a high spur of the main Alleghany; and the valley of Howard's creek divides them from the Greenbrier mountains opposite.

ANVIL ROCK, GREENBRIER RIVER.

JUNCTION OF GREENBRIER AND NEW RIVERS.

in peace and war—and of pleasant memory in connection with the old Supreme Court of Virginia, which held regular sessions at this court-house. The town is beautifully located in a depression of the Greenbrier hills, and is the centre of a highly cultivated vicinage—with fruit, wheat and stock farms, and the best of grazing lands.

RONCEVERTE STATION,

237 miles from Richmond, and on the bank of Greenbrier River, is one of the most important lumber stations of the line.

The St. Lawrence Boom and Manufacturing Company have here their saw-mills, ice piers, log booms, and other provision for a large lumber business.

Ronceverte is the business depot of Lewisburg and of the fine farming country around.

West of Ronceverte is the Second Creek tunnel, 1,550 feet in length, and excavated through limestone rock. At the western portal of this tunnel, the railroad makes its second crossing of the Greenbrier River— again with an iron bridge.

FORT SPRING,

244 miles from Richmond, is the point of shipment for Union, the county seat of Monroe county, 12 miles distant. This country is the southward continuation of the Greenbrier limestone belt, with its pleasant aspect and all the productive characteristics of this high and healthy region. A considerable traffic comes to the railroad from Fort Spring

and other depots of the Greenbrier district, in live stock, grain, butter and country produce generally.

The Fort Spring quarries supply a superior limestone (92 per cent. carbonate of lime) for the Quinnimont Iron Furnace, 42 miles westward.

Dade's tunnel, 1,150 feet long, is immediately west of Fort Spring station.

ALDERSON,

251 miles from Richmond, and 1,550 feet above tide-level, is a thriving village, of railroad origin and growth; and with fine farming country around, on both sides of the Greenbrier River.

An excellent quality of lumber is shipped from the Boa and Mohler mills of Alderson, both east and west.

AT LOWELL STATION

the Chesapeake and Ohio Railroad makes its third and last crossing of Greenbrier River, over an iron bridge of 543 feet in length.

Lowell is an important shipping point for live stock from South-Western Virginia. Westward, the limestone of the middle section of the Greenbrier Valley gives place to the sandstones and shales of the sub-carboniferous formation.

TALCOTT,

two miles beyond, is the stage station for the Red Sulphur Springs of Monroe county, distant 12 miles.

One mile westward is the eastern portal of the Great Bend tunnel, 6,400 feet in length, and driven through the shale rocks of the formation. This work saves a detour of eight miles by the Geeenbrier River; and from the summit of the tunnel, 470 feet above the grade line, is one of the finest views of the upper Greenbrier Valley. Though the largest tunnel on the line, it was completed in time to avoid temporary tracks or other expedients often required to pass the heavier work of new railroads. Only two shafts were used in its construction.

HINTON,

273 miles from Richmond, and 1,377 feet above the sea, is prettily situated at the confluence of the Greenbrier and New Rivers. It is the county seat of Summers county and a place of growing importance.

From Hinton, 67 miles up New River to the Atlantic, Mississippi and Ohio railroad, there is partial bateau navigation, for the improvement of which the United States

Congress has passed appropriations. Surveys have also been made for a good railroad location, and when constructed, this line will be an important feeder to the Chesapeake and Ohio Railroad—for rich iron ores are found in quantity in Giles county, 35 to 40 miles above Hinton, which can only be profitably reduced with the Chesapeake and Ohio coal and cokes. The nearest coke ovens, now completed, are at Quinnimont, 21 miles west, but still nearer sites may be found.

At Hinton are located the engine houses and coaling stations of this division, and a short distance below are the ballast quarries and crushers.

The picturesque and graceful views of the Greenbrier Valley here gradually change to scenery of bolder and rougher characteristics; and lower down the New River gorge to the wild grandeur of the American canons.

For several miles west of Hinton, the river views from the rear platform of the car present a pleasing contrast of rock, cliff and river ripple, of wooded slopes and graceful hill outlines—the river almost imperceptibly narrowing its width. Above Hinton the low water width of New River exceeds 1,000 feet. Forty-five miles below, and with many intermediate affluents, that width is reduced to 75 feet and less, and with no increased depth or velocity of current sufficient to explain this great change of water section. The boulders around suggest the character of the river-bed. Duly considering this, let the thinking traveller study out a problem not yet determined by the best authorities.

Seven miles west of Hinton, the New River suddenly plunges over the New River Falls. For a river of this width, the word "cascade" is certainly a misnomer. Yet with a vertical fall of but 24 feet, (rapids included) the more pretentious word "cataract" magnifies. Words aside, this waterfall is most pleasingly remembered among the charmingly beautiful views of this favored and much admired route for the tourist; and no less, before railroad times, by the genial followers of old Izaak Walton.

In studying the peculiar characteristics of the New and Kanawha rivers, the hydraulic engineer will compare with interest the volume of water poured over the New River Falls with that of the Kanawha Falls, 54 miles below; although between the two, the Gauley River and many considerable affluents contribute their flow—at times, very large. The New River Falls supply one of the best manufacturing sites and most valuable water-powers upon the line of these rivers.

NEW RIVER FALLS STATION,

two miles on, is the nearest depot to the Green Sulphur Springs, a pretty spot six miles up the Lick Creek Valley. The Beury powder mill is on the same creek, one half mile from the railroad.

MEADOW CREEK,

three miles west, and Paw-Paw five miles further, are points of shipment for a considerable amount of choice oak, poplar and walnut timber (generally in square logs) to the Eastern cities and to Europe; also stave and assorted timber, hoop-poles and locust tree-nails.

RUNNING NEW RIVER RAPIDS.

"THE NEW RIVER FALLS."

·III.

THE COAL FIELDS.

Near the line of Little Meadow creek, 285 miles from Richmond, and 1,265 feet above the sea, the Chesapeake and Ohio railroad enters the great carboniferous formation of North America, extending from Alabama, through North Georgia, East Tennessee and Kentucky, West Virginia and Eastern Ohio, into Pennsylvania and nearly to the New York line.

The New River and Kanawha valleys cross this vast coal field, on the line of its greatest breadth, in a winding course, through its best and purest coals; and exposing their geological sections for an average vertical depth of over 1,000 feet. Built down these valleys, the Chesapeake and Ohio railroad supplies not only the outlet to market, but being located along the base of the enclosing mountains, it presents, with its branch tracks, exceptional facilities for the economical operation of the mines above. The traveller in passing these mines (at once recognized by their inclines and other simple expedients for delivering coal into the railroad cars) will notice the suggestive absence of all pumping, ventilating and elevating machinery—for drainage and transportation can here be arranged, almost without exception, by gravity. Shaft work, so generally a very heavy charge in coal mining elsewhere, is unknown in this district, except for occasional air-holes, sunk at small cost. Also the coal seams being nearly horizontal, and the surface depressions permitting cheap and easy ventilation, there is a notable exemption from mine accidents: no life has been lost, and no serious casualty has been reported in the mines of the Chesapeake and Ohio road, from their opening up to the date of this paper (1878).

The New River and Kanawha coal measures are no less remarkable for their extent, variety, quality and commercial value than for the very low cost of opening and operating the mines.

AT QUINNIMONT STATION,

294 miles from Richmond, and 1,196 feet above tide-level, is the first coal mining enterprise met in travelling westward.

Directly at the depot is a large iron furnace (16' x 60') with improved machinery and complete equipment for the production of iron on a large scale and at low cost; and with the surroundings of a pretty mountain village.

One mile from the railroad, up Laurel creek, are the coal mines and coke ovens which supply this furnace, and with full arrangements to ship all surplus production. At the mines, (on the mountain slopes, 900 feet vertically above the ovens, 80 in number) will be observed simple appliances to pass coal by gravity from the mine-breast through all stages of manipulation, until it is delivered an excellent coke on the stock-house floor of the furnace, one and a fourth miles distant.

The ores used come from mines, or "banks," east of the Alleghany mountains, as heretofore stated, and the limestone flux from the Greenbrier quarries. There is a fair limestone, two and half miles, rough wagon haul, from the furnace; but the railroad facilities for cheap movement and convenient delivery within the furnace stockhouse, soon decided the question of comparative economy.

Before the opening of the Chesapeake and Ohio Railroad this "mouth of Laurel," or Quinnimont, was one of the wildest and most inaccessible recesses of the New River Valley or gorge. Here was planted an enterprise, to test the economic value of the New River coals and coke used in combination with the hematite ores, 100 miles distant, of Augusta, Rockbridge and Alleghany counties, (Va.) It was prosecuted through a commercial pressure which has suspended over one half of the iron furnaces of the United States, and it now presents an example of what persistence and business determination, combined with great natural advantages, can accomplish under difficulties.

The Quinnimont furnace was put in blast in the fall of 1874; with intervals for repairs, &c., it has been operated almost ever since. The superior quality of this iron commands the highest market rates, for foundry grades, from Pittsburgh to St. Louis; and eastward, it competes with "Scotch Pig" for finer castings.

STRETCHER'S NECK TUNNEL,

one mile west, and 1,900 feet in length, passes the railroad through a salient spur of the Big Sewell mountain range, which abuts on (or is cut through by) the New River from a point some distance above the "War-Ridge" of Quinnimont, to the vicinity of Sewell station, below. The scenery of this strange valley

continues to grow rougher and more wildly picturesque, as the railroad penetrates its lower passes; and very plainly shows indications of the powerful forces, erosive or otherwise, which cut or wore this valley so deeply into the clays, shales, coals and the softer rocks of the formation—also undermining the heavy sandstone bluffs above and precipitating their huge boulder masses down the slopes and into the river below. Quoting again the writer in Batchelder:

"At Sewell, formerly known as Boyer's Ferry, forty miles below the mouth of the Greenbrier, the valley becomes a true canon. For twenty miles below there is not a strip of arable land in the valley, and at points the cliffs are perpendicular from the river edge. Here the scenery is wild indeed. Such slopes as these are generally covered with boulders, some of immense size; and

"BIG DOWDY" FALLS.

WHITCOMB'S BOULDER.

along these slopes and under frowning cliffs the railroad gropes its way under their shadow; one of which, "Whitcomb's boulder," it was proposed to tunnel as the easiest solution of a location of the road, and it was actually under-cut on one side for trains to pass. The passenger looks upward a thousand feet or more as the train sweeps a graceful curve around some concave bend, and sees the beetling cliffs of many colored sandstone, looking with their great angles like gigantic castles and fortresses erected by nature to guard these her penetralia."

BUFFALO AND DIMMOCK STATIONS

are in the heart of the New River coal basin, with outcrops of the several seams appearing on both sides of the river.

AT FIRE CREEK,

310 miles from Richmond, are the mines of the "Fire Creek Coal and Coke Company," which ship east and west a first-class coal for steamers and smith's use. Thirty coke ovens have already been completed to meet the furnace and foundry demand of the line; and preparation has been made for an increase.

AT SEWELL STATION,

three miles on, are the mines of the Longdale Coal and Iron Company, which supply coke for their Alleghany furnace, before mentioned. Their forty coke ovens, built directly upon the Chesapeake and Ohio track, present a good example of the better oven construction and management.

AT NUTTALLBURG,

317 miles from Richmond, the Nuttall mines supply coal for the Old Dominion line of steamers between Richmond and New York; and supplied the Russian fleet when, last year, in Hampton Roads. The Nuttall coke is sent to furnaces on the Ohio River chiefly.

FAYETTE STATION

is the depot of Fayetteville (C. H.,) two miles distant, The coal seams of the vicinity have here been tested and partially opened, but are not yet regularly mined.

AT HAWK'S NEST,

324 miles from Richmond, and 828 feet above the sea, the Beury & Williams mine is in operation, with a small number of coke ovens completed; and three miles up Mill creek, by branch track, the Gauley Mountain mines are shipping to eastern cities. The Hawks-nest coke is consumed by furnaces on the line.

The Chesapeake and Ohio Railroad here crosses New River on a fine iron bridge, 669 feet in length, and of engineering interest from the successful foundations for its masonry, which were secured on the boulders in the bed of the torrent. The cut on page 26 gives a bird's-eye-view of this bridge-crossing and the gorge above.

THE HAWKS-NEST CLIFFS,

600 feet vertically above the railroad, and on the crest of which passes the old James River and Kanawha turnpike, have long been points of note to the tourist, From this point to Cotton Hill and the Kanawha Falls, are some of the most beautiful views and striking scenery of this region. The railroad location is here especially bold, and will arrest the attention of experts, as before upon the Greenbrier division, from its thorough study and skill. The cliff excavation of these sections was one of the earliest

applications in America of nitro-glycerine, as an explosive for difficult rock-work.

KANAWHA FALLS,

immediately below the junction of New and Gauley rivers, marks the head of the Great Kanawha River. These falls are more beautiful than imposing. They are widely known as a very pleasant fishing resort.

KANAWHA FALLS STATION

is 333 miles from Richmond and 672 feet above the sea. The New River at this point (where it becomes the Kanawha) entirely changes its character—from the mountain torrent of many miles back, to a gentle, beautiful stream, partaking of the general characteristics of the Ohio affluents.

Between the Hawk's Nest and the Kanawha Falls there is also a great change in the coal formation. The "lower measures" of the New River section, which at Quinnimont are over 1,000 feet above the river-level, with their continuous north-westward dip, now pass under New River; and westward, above water-level, we have the Kanawha section proper, comprising the rich cannel, splint and gas coals of this remarkable group. In the vicinity of Armstrong creek, where the "Ansted" measurements were taken, at Cannelton, and at Morris, Upper, Paint and Cabin creeks, are exposed the finest vertical sections of the Kanawha coals—averaging from 40 to 50 feet of solid coal, in workable seams, occasionally ten feet thick. Transversely to the axis of dip, these seams can be worked horizontally to the extreme limits of the district, with few faults, and with drainage, as stated, by gravity, except where some simple syphon arrangement is used for occasional rolls or waves.

AT CANNELTON STATION,

343 miles from Richmond, there are ten good mines along the railroad and on the Morris creek branch-track, within a radius of two miles from the depot, viz: the Stone and Wyant, Faulkner, W. R. Johnson (Crescent), the Coal Valley, Straughan (with coke ovens), Kanawha Coal Company, Old

FERN SPRING BRANCH.

Virginia Colliery, Eureka, Morris Creek Crescent, and the Lewiston-Kanawha Company. These mines ship a superior quality of gas coal, in demand in the coal markets of New York, Boston and other eastern cities; besides supplying the gas-works of Richmond and other Virginia cities. Their block coal is much esteemed for grate and engine use.

On the opposite bank of the Kanawha River, the Cannelton Company mine largely a cannel coal of very high repute as a gas enricher; also from other seams on the same property, the Caking (Coal Valley), the semi-cannel and block. These coals are ferried across for shipment by the Chesapeake and Ohio Railroad, in advance of the construction of a bridge to be built to serve the valuable properties on the same bank of the Kanawha, and for that reason still undeveloped. The outcrops of cannel coal, especially, and of splint and gas, on Staten Run and Upper Hughes' creek, are notable

MILLER'S FERRY FROM THE HAWK'S NEST.

nous mines, connecting with the railroad by a branch track. Thence to the vicinity of Charleston there are several mines and coal openings along the railroad, worked irregularly for the salt furnaces and local consumption.

NEAR SPRING HILL STATION,

375 miles from Richmond, a branch track has been graded up Davis' creek to the fine coals of that valley. At the head of the same creek and on the slopes of Briar creek beyond, are the Blackband ore seams (almost indentical in analysis with the Scotch blackband) and needing only the completion of this branch-track to become a valuable source of supply for the iron furnaces of the Chesapeake and Ohio Railroad.

ST. ALBAN'S STATION,

six miles on, and the mouth of Coal River, is the outlet of another large and valuable sub-division of the great coal-field. It is from that point the Peytona Company ship their very superior cannel coals, east to New York and New England, and west to Cincinnati and the cities of the Ohio River Valley.

Beyond Scary station (385 miles from Richmond and 590 feet above the sea) the Chesapeake and Ohio Railroad leaves the Kanawha Valley. Thence to the Kentucky State line, it skirts the northern outcrop of the Guyandotte and the Big Sandy coal-fields; and by branch tracks, it is their only outlet eastward by rail.

for extent and quality, among the best of the district.

AT PAINT CREEK STATION,

five miles below, are the Doddridge, and Gordon and Seal mines—gray splint; at Blacksburg, (Mason Hoge and Mason)—rich gas coal; also the Ault mine at Hampton city adjoining.

AT COALBURG,

353 miles from Richmond, the Robinson and the Stuart Buck (East-bank) ship a superior splint coal, both east and west. The Coalmont and Red House mines are three miles on.

NEAR BROWNSTOWN,

360 miles from Richmond, are the Brownstown Company's cannel and semi-bitumi-

The Kanawha coal trade may still be considered to be in its earlier development. Prior to the opening of the Chesapeake and Ohio Railroad in 1873, the Kanawha River, with its unreliable and imperfect navigation, was the only outlet of this coal-field; and that only in one direction. Since 1873, the coal mines along the Chesapeake and Ohio Railroad have increased, year by year, in number; and through the liberal and fostering policy of that company in freight charges, there has been a very large increase in its coal tonnage, viz: 1874, total shipment 158,716 tons (2,000 lbs.); 1875, 231,717 tons; 1876, 264,386 tons; and in 1877, 310,352 tons.

THE KANAWHA VALLEY.

Kanawha, in the Indian, means "river of the woods," probably so called from the magnificent timber of this district, of which a portion still remains; and in its full original growth, upon many of the tributaries. The valley of the Great Kanawha from the falls to the Ohio River, is one of positive beauty. Hills with irregular crest, averaging in height 700 feet above the stream, enclose this valley with ever changing and very graceful outlines. Between the well wooded slopes of these hills, is spread, in pleasing contrast, a fertile river bottom never less than one half mile in width and frequently much greater. But for its mining and salt industries, the Kanawha Valley would be better known in agriculture and more in connection with its very attractive surroundings.

The Kanawha history is interesting. At Point Pleasant, where that stream enters the Ohio, was fought (1774) the desperate battle which decided the white supremacy of the Ohio Valley—the Colonial forces commanded by Andrew Lewis and the Indians by their chief, Cornplanter. Indian relics abound in the valley, reminding us that it was one of their favorite resting places—and well worth a death struggle. The accompanying cut, of one of the Indian mounds, is suggestive in this connection.

From the falls down to Charleston, the Kanawha Valley is studded with villages— Cannelton, Clifton, Hampton, Coalburg, Lewiston, Brownstown, the Salines, Alden with its chemical works, and Salton, on the left bank; and opposite, Malden, the Campbell's Creek mines, Snow Hill, the Brook's furnace and other salt works.

CHARLESTON,

369 miles by rail from Richmond and 602 feet above sea-level (railroad grade) is the

THE HAWK'S NEST, FROM BOULDER POINT.

commercial centre of the Kanawha Valley; and by a recent vote of the State, it is to be the Capital of West Virginia. It is a well built city of about 4,500 inhabitants, pleasantly situated on the east bank of the Kanawha, at its confluence with the Elk River.

The most important industries of the vicinity are the mining operations—and especially coal—which contribute largely to the business of the city. The Kanawha salt production, though much depressed by the times, is still important. In the State Centennial Report, Dr. J. P. Hale gives a list of ten furnaces of 2,500,000 bushels capacity, but at present worked to less than half duty. Bromine and other chemical works are operated in connection with the Alden Wells.

SNOW HILL SALT WORKS

The lumber trade of Charleston is considerable, calling for five saw mills in and around the city; and pump and barrel factories. There are also woollen and flour mills, iron foundries and machine works; and in West Charleston, an iron blast furnace not yet completed.

Petroleum has long been known in the Kanawha Salines. It was pumped up with the brine, but from the greater value of the latter in times past, was wasted or "tubed out." The failure of oil wells in other localities has turned attention seriously to this field. Several borings are now in progress near Charleston, and while oil has not yet been found in "flowing" quantities, still enough has been pumped to warrant the further prosecution of these operations.

LEAVING THE KANAWHA VALLEY,

by the slopes of Scary creek, the Chesapeake and Ohio Railroad ascends with gentle grades, and traverses for nearly thirty miles the intervening rolling country, which occasionally rises to a height of 80 feet above track-level opposite Charleston.

SCOTT, HURRICANE AND MILTON STATIONS

are the principal points of shipment for this district, from which comes a handsome and steadily increasing local business. There will be observed around these stations decided evidences of the development of this country which has followed the opening of the railroad.

BARBOURSVILLE,

410 miles from Richmond, is the county seat of Cabell county, and the centre of a fertile farming district along, and between, the Guyandotte and Mud River valleys.

GUYANDOTTE,

seven miles on, and at the mouth of the river of the same name, was the steamboat station for the old time stage travel which crossed the mountains by the James River and Kanawha turnpike. A considerable logging and timber trade comes down this river, and the rich outcrops of the Guyandotte coal field are not far distant from the line of the railroad.

INCLINE PLAIN AT CANNELTON.

CHARLESTON—THE WEST VIRGINIA CAPITAL.

HUNTINGTON

was laid off in 1871; and settled since the opening of the Western division of the railroad. In 1872 it assumed something of the appearance indicated in the accompanying cut; and for sometime after its growth was rapid. In the fall of 1873, came the commercial panic, which prostrated the country and suspended, for a time, in common with other leading public improvements, the western connections of the Chesapeake and Ohio

CROSSING THE GUYANDOTTE RIVER,

the railroad enters the Ohio Valley proper, in one of its fairest, and in every way most attractive sections. For twelve miles down to the Big Sandy River (on the Kentucky State line) there is a beautiful stretch of the celebrated "bottom lands" which figured so largely in the later Colonial history; and the permanent possession of which so intensified the Indian struggle.

Upon the upper and more elevated portion of this plateau, which rises gradually from high water mark on the river bank to the slopes of the enclosing hills, is located the city of Huntington—the terminus on the Ohio of the Chesapeake and Ohio Railroad, 421 miles from the navigable waters of the James River and 568 feet above sea or tide level.*

INDIAN MOUND, NEAR ST. ALBANS.

* These terms have been used indiscriminately, as their difference in the lower James River is slight.

HUNTINGTON AND THE OHIO RIVER.

Railroad. Notwithstanding, Huntington continued to grow; and in 1878, the City Recorder states: "Population about 3,000, and increasing; large saw mills, planing and flour mills and furniture factory; Ensign Car-wheel and Manufacturing works; Bank of Huntington; newspapers and printing offices, stores, hotels and a public hall; Marshall College (State normal school) with library and scientific apparatus, and from 125 to 150 students; three public schools, five churches; and fifteen miles of streets (80 feet wide), and avenues for drives, opened and graded; public cisterns for use in case of fires; a cemetery of ten acres, laid out and improved. Taxation low, and no city debt. "

In addition to the above, it may be added that any one walking through the Huntington streets (for little is seen from the cars) will find many handsome residences and the principal structures of the place well built in brick and stone : and a stroll along the water-front, five miles on the Ohio and Guyandotte rivers, will at once suggest why this site was selected for the terminus of such a railroad.

Huntington is favorably situated for the manufactures sucessfully prosecuted in the west, and especially those using coal, iron and fine timber. Already coal and coke brought by the Chesapeake and Ohio Railroad is constantly shipped from Huntington to the older furnaces and forges of Ironton and Cincinnati; also iron ores from Lowmoor and other Chesapeake and Ohio mines pass through Huntington furnaces from Wheeling to Newport (Ky.) opposite Cincinnati. It is consequently simply a question of time when the same ores and fuel will stop in Huntington, for reduction there; and especially when the "black band" and other local ores shall have been made cheaply accessible. The Ensign Car-Wheel and Manufacturing Works, with their excellent plant, are the pioneers of others.

The Chesapeake and Ohio Railroad Company have erected, in the upper part of Huntington, extensive machine and car shops, engine houses and accessory buildings of handsome design and substantial execution—planned for extension as the increasing road traffic may demand for the mechanical wants of the western division of the road.

In approaching and passing Huntington the railroad was located with reference to its western connections. In the rear of

Huntington, and near its western limits, a handsome passenger depot has been built for the Junction Station. The main track continues westward, and the river track curves north on the line of approach to the projected railroad bridge over the Ohio River. This Huntington crossing, from its good foundations, stone quarries and other bridge essentials, is considered one of the best between Pittsburgh and Cincinnati. So direct is the course of this reach of the Ohio River, that steamboats and their tows will have the bridge in full sight for several miles, up and down.

Reaching the river bank, the track returns eastward to the steamboat landings and the wharf boats, where also are located the freight depot and sheds, the inclines and other appliances for the rapid transfer of heavy freights by steam power.

The western passenger connections of the Chesapeake and Ohio Railroad are maintained through the Huntington and Cincinnati Steam Packet Line—a very pleasant and acceptable change in long travel. There is also daily connection by steamboat with the cities and towns of the Upper Ohio.

Through connections by rail, with all the Western railroad systems, are not now far distant in time. From Huntington to Portsmouth (where rail communication has been secured with Columbus and Chicago by the Scioto Valley Railroad) but forty-six miles of light line remaining to be built, and a company has been organized to close the gap—possibly during the present year. Also in the direction of Kentucky, but eighty-eight miles of road are required between the Big Sandy and Mount Sterling to connect with Lexington, Louisville and the railroad systems of the Southwest; and a direct line of railroad, down the Ohio Valley to Cincinnati, is in the near future.

The experience of the past three years, however, has attested the value of the Ohio water line to the Chesapeake and Ohio Railroad—especially in the transportation of grain in bulk, of tobacco, cotton, live-stock, coal-oil and all produce from the West: and of ores, coal, coke from its own line—and general merchandise from Eastern cities—both seeking the line of least cost westward.

It is by no means certain that the productive and commercial capacities of the Ohio Valley, have even now been fully appreciated or tested. The Chesapeake and Ohio Railroad, with its low grades and its ability to move heavy freights at very low cost, will be a most important element in the future determination of this question.

CLIMATE.

The climate of the region traversed by the Chesapeake and Ohio Railroad has long attracted attention, being mild, very healthy and especially favorable for agriculture. During 1876 and 1877 the average temperature for each month was as follows:—

SIGNAL SERVICE BUREAU OBSERVATION.—AT 7.35 A. M.

	RICHMOND.		WHITE SULPHUR.		HINTON.		HUNTINGTON.	
	1876.	1877.	1876.	1877.	1876.	1877.	1876.	1877.
JANUARY	40°	27°	31°	25°	33°	22°	41°	31°
FEBRUARY	42	35	29	31	31	37	34	37
MARCH	39	35	29	33	32	34	35	42
APRIL	48	53	35	38	45	45	46	51
MAY	57	60	55	55	56	53	58	60
JUNE	70	75	69	58	65	66	70	69
JULY	71	79	70	65	72	73	74	80
AUGUST	72	75	67	67	69	67	71	75
SEPTEMBER	65	66	57	61	60	60	62	72
OCTOBER	48	58	45	46	43	50	45	52
NOVEMBER	43	47	40	36	39	39	42	39
DECEMBER	36	44	20	35	22	36	25	40

ROUTES AND RESORTS ON CHESAPEAKE & OHIO RAILWAY.

FROM NEW ENGLAND, CANADA & NEW YORK,

take the New York and Washington Through Line *via* Gordonsville, or Old Dominion Steamship Route from New York *via* Richmond.

FROM CENTRAL & WESTERN NEW YORK & PENNSYLVANIA,

take the routes *via* Washington and Gordonsville; or the York River Line from Baltimore *via* Richmond.

AT WASHINGTON,

take the Virginia Midland trains at B. and P. depot *via* Gordonsville.

FROM THE WESTERN PORTION OF THE MIDDLE STATES,

take the route *via* Harper's Ferry, Shenandoah Valley and Staunton.

FROM NORFOLK, OLD POINT COMFORT & THE EASTERN SHORE,

take the Atlantic, Mississippi and Ohio Route *via* Petersburg and Richmond; or the Virginia Steamboat Line *via* James River and Richmond.

FROM THE SOUTHERN ATLANTIC STATES,

take the Piedmont Air-Line, or Atlantic Coast Line *via* Richmond.

FROM THE TENNESSEE LINE & SOUTHWEST VIRGINIA,

take the route *via* Lynchburg and Charlottesville.

FROM THE CENTRAL & WESTERN STATES,

take the routes *via* Cincinnati and Huntington.

FROM CENTRAL & NORTHERN OHIO,

take the Scioto valley route *via* Portsmouth and Huntington.

FROM THE OHIO RIVER POINTS,

take the Chesapeake and Ohio trains at Huntington.

At the connecting point, (Richmond, Gordonsville, Charlottesville, Staunton or Huntington,) the passenger takes the Chesapeake and Ohio train and leaves it at the springs' station, mentioned on his ticket, taking one of the stage coaches or carriages, which await the arrival of the trains, to the watering place or resort selected.

The Chesapeake and Ohio Railway, between Richmond and Huntington, 421 miles, is possessed of superior appliancies for safety and comfort in its smooth track, and best motive power and is equipped with elegant brakes and all other modern improvements.

THROUGH SLEEPERS RUN BETWEEN RICHMOND AND WHITE SULPHUR.

THROUGH SLEEPERS ON NIGHT TRAINS AND PARLOR CARS ON DAY TRAINS RUN, *via* Gordonsville, between Washington and White Sulphur.

Straight and Round-Trip Tickets, good until November first, and including transportation between C. & O. stations and springs, (except White Sulphur,) are on sale at all principal ticket offices.

CHESAPEAKE & OHIO RAILWAY.

IV.

VIRGINIA SPRINGS AND MOUNTAIN RESORTS.

Summer resorts have become a recognized necessity of modern society. The keen competition in business and consequent intensity of occupation and feverish excitement of those engaged in it—the incessant activity of professional men—and the artificial life led by all classes and both sexes in our cities, call for a period of rest, relaxation and recreation.

According to the fable of antiquity, Hercules could not, at first, conquer Antæus (who was the son of Earth and Sea) because each time the giant was thrown to the ground he gained new strength from mother Earth. The parallel is easily drawn: the fable needs no labored interpretation. As the human mind and body need sleep—as they should have one day in seven for rest—so do they require, each year, a period during which they may escape from the toils and complications of business, the hot breath of the cities, and—out of seeming evil educing good—gain new vigor for the battle of life by simple contact with mother Earth—breathing the air, using the diet, seeing the sights, and hearing the sounds of the country.

The Summer resorts on the line of the Chesapeake and Ohio Railway, as will be seen, comprise every variety, from the famous "Mecca," where fashion's votaries make their yearly pilgrimage, to the quiet retreat where families find Summer homes. The ball-room, music, bowling-alleys, billiard-rooms, croquet grounds, and all of the many appliances to furnish pastimes to the pleasure seeker, as well as waters which possess healing efficacy for every infirmity to which the human frame is subject, are found at the Virginia Springs.

Last, and not least, for invalid and pleasure-seeker, at every fashionable watering-place and every quiet retreat, scenery of rare beauty and air unsurpassed for healthfulness are found by those who, guided by these pages, visit the places described.

As showing the impressions produced upon the traveller by the magnificent scenery of this route, we append the following extracts from a letter of the Rev. John Hall, D. D., published in the *New York Ledger*, and entitled,

"A PEEP INTO THE VIRGINIAS."

"My way lay along the line of the Chesapeake and Ohio Railroad, and he who can travel by it unmoved ought to be placed permanently on the Jersey flats, and forbidden the sight of anything more picturesque than a machine-shop. There is a famous road in Italy which attracts by its rapid alternations of dark tunnel and picturesque valley; but it is no exaggeration to say that as much could be abstracted from the Virginian line without being missed. Every one who ever crossed the Alps into Italy, remembers the zigzags from which he looks down on the valley he is reaching. But the hills around are bare and hard. The generous Alleghanies and the Blue Ridge are richly wooded to their tops, and look as soft and green as the hill-sides around Lake Maggiore. All travellers by the Pennsylvania Central remember that attractive piece of fancy engineering known as the horse-shoe, and nobody has gone to California without recalling the doubling of Cape Horn—where your train winds round the high brow of a mountain, as if it had climbed up to give you a look at the valleys below. The traveller across the Virginias can have delights like these again and again repeated. The Rhine owes no little of its attractiveness to the battlements on its steeps. The New River is not indeed like the Rhine in depth or breadth; but it has features of its own. Now it is a broad stream leisurely chattering to the woods that overhang it; anon it is in a narrower bed scolding the rocks as large as houses, that have intruded themselves upon it from the hillsides, of which they grew weary. But for giant cliffs, Eagle's Nests, Lover's Leaps, Drachenfels, and mountain fastnesses in ruins, the New River can compete with any stream of travelled lands, and with this difference in its favor, that no cunning count or baron bold piled up those frowning battlements. Geological forces in an Omnipotent hand, and with unlimited time in which to work, placed these precipitous, castle-like crowns on the wooded hills, and gave them a peculiarity not seen elsewhere, namely, that behind them corn and wine abound ; for the Alleghanies are fertile to their summits. As one is whirled along, it is difficult to say which challenges most admiration—the river below, the cliffs above, the graceful lines of the hills, the moving shadows over the green slopes of the mountain sides, or the sublime audacity that dared to run a railroad through such a region.

But so much needs to be said about the picturesque that there is danger of overlooking the salt works, the marble, the iron works, the coal-mines that one notices on his way, and which, long trains of freight-cars respectfully waiting on sidings to let him pass, will not allow him to forget. There is no waste in the world's wide domain, and these mountains, like those of a better known land, are iron, and out of them man may dig richer minerals than the brass of the olden time. The work is begun. As in all great enterprises that affect the world, the earliest race of workers may reap but little of the reward, possibly ; but some time men will see the gain, and admire the energy and skill that clasped the Virginias in iron bands between the open sea-board and the Great West."

The following details concerning the

VIRGINIA SPRINGS AND SUMMER RESORTS

are given in the order in which their localities are reached by the traveller from Richmond, and without relation to their respective social, remedial or other attractions.

THE MECHUM'S RIVER HOUSE,

situated at the Depot of the same name, ten miles west of Charlottesville and 107 miles from Richmond, has accommodations for forty or fifty persons, and is a favorite resort for families during the Summer months. The spacious and well shaded grounds make it especially attractive to children. Its proximity to the cities, and situation immediately on the railroad, make it particularly desirable for the families of persons who can only spare a few days at a time from their business.

THE GREENWOOD HOUSE,

like those at Mechum's River and Afton, is a favorite resort to those desiring accessibility, pure air and moderate terms. It is immediately on the Chesapeake and Ohio Railroad, at Greenwood station, 115 miles from Richmond, and is a pleasant and cool retreat for families with children.

THE AFTON HOUSE

is a summer resort, immediately on the Chesapeake and Ohio Railroad, at Afton depot, 120 miles from Richmond, and "cannot be surpassed for easy access, dry, pure air, splendid views and healthy location; being situated on one of the spurs of the Blue Ridge mountains, the breeze is almost continuous."

THE MOUNTAIN-TOP HOUSE

is two miles from Afton depot, on the top of

PLEASURE (?) TRAVEL IN THE OLDEN TIME.

the Blue Ridge mountain, immediately over the long tunnel of the Chesapeake and Ohio Railway. The place is 1,996 feet above sea-level, and much resorted to by families for a cool and quiet retreat; the mercury rarely rising above 72° at any time. Visitors, by giving previous information to the conductor of their desire to do so, can leave the *day-trains* at the west-end of the "Blue Ridge tunnel," half mile from the mountain-Top House.

STAUNTON, VA.,

136 miles from Richmond, occupies a delightfully elevated position at the head of the Shenandoah Valley, between the lofty Blue Ridge on the east and on the west the still loftier range of the Alleghany mountains, and is a most agreeable place of residence as well as of Summer resort. It is a favorite point of stoppage with Summer tourists on their way to the mineral springs of Virginia. This is the point of departure for

THE STRIBLING (AUGUSTA) SPRINGS,

only thirteen miles distant, by a romantic stage road, and a favorite resort to many who year after year seek these healing waters and enjoyable accommodations. Several different mineral waters, alum, sulphur and chalybeate, offer their remedial virtues for various classes of deseases.

WEYER'S CAVE

is in Augusta county, sixteen miles from Staunton, and easily reached either by the Valley Railroad to Cave station, thence four miles by stage to the cave; or by *livery* from Staunton direct to the cave. It derives its name from Bernard Weyer, who discovered it in 1804 while in pursuit of a wild animal that took refuge in it. Dr. Moorman in his "Virginia Springs" thus writes of it: "It would be difficult to convey an adequate idea of the vastness and sublimity of some, or the exquisite beauty and grandeur of others, of its innumerable apartments, with their snowy-white concretions of a thousand various forms. Weyer's cave is one of the great natural wonders of this New World, and for its eminence in its own class, deserves to be ranked with the Natural Bridge and Niagara. Its length, by the most direct course, is more than 1,600 feet, and by the more winding paths twice that distance; and its objects are remarkable for their variety, formation and beauty." A writer in *Scribner's Magazine* describes it as "a vast sub-terranean labyrinth of glittering grottos and iridescent galleries, where stalactites of extraordinary brilliancy sparkle in the torch-light, and hang from the fretted roof like the corbels and foliated pendants of a gothic cathedral. Here are pulpits and organs, audience chambers and throne rooms; here the ceaseless petrifaction takes all manner of beautiful and fantastic shapes, throwing its drapery around the form of a vestal or fastening its jewels to the person of a queen, as the visitor passes along its crystal colonnades and stops delighted before its frozen cataracts." Within a few hundred yards of Weyer's cave is Madison's cave, or the

"CAVE OF FOUNTAINS,"

which extends three hundred feet into the earth and branches into numerous subordinate caverns. The vault is from twenty to fifty feet high, through which water is continually trickling down and encrusting the sides with crystalline forms of elegant drapery.

THE VARIETY SPRINGS,

so called from the several different mineral springs on the grounds, are immediately on the Chesapeake and Ohio Railroad, at Variety station, sixteen miles from Staunton, and a very pleasant retreat for healthfulness and quiet rest.

THE CRAWFORD SPRINGS,

one mile from Pond Gap station, and 155 miles from Richmond, are located immediately at the base of Elliotts Knob, the highest point of the mountains of Virginia. The waters of the main spring are sulphur, and at a short distance is a chalybeate spring, the waters of which are supplied to guests. This is a delightfully cool and pleasant retreat during the hot Summer months.

THE GOSHEN HOTEL

is at the station of the same name, 168 miles from Richmond, and a pleasant place to spend the hot season, or to rest before taking the stages for the Cold Sulphur, Rockbridge Baths, Lexington, Natural Bridge, Rockbridge Alum and Jordan Alum. Situated in a little valley through which passes the Cow Pasture River, constant breezes refresh the traveller and visitor during the hottest days.

THE COLD SULPHUR SPRINGS,

two miles from Goshen depot, Chesapeake and Ohio Railroad, is a delightful and popular Summer retreat, in the Virginia mountains. The waters are light tonic and adapted to the most delicate constitutions, and are

SPRING HOUSE—ROCKBRIDGE ALUM SPRINGS, VA.

use. The North River, which flows by the lawn, affords excellent sport to those fond of fishing and rowing, in addition to the usual round of balls and gayeties for the pleasure seeking visitor.

The road continuing, leads the traveller on to the town of Lexington, eleven miles from the Baths, which is chiefly interesting as the site of the Virginia Military Institute and the Washington-Lee University, of which Gen. R. E. Lee was president, and in whose chapel basement himself, his wife and daughter lie buried. Gen. T. J. Jackson also is buried at Lexington, in the Presbyterian burying ground.

Fourteen miles beyond Lexington is the famous

NATURAL BRIDGE,

thirty-six miles from Goshen, which, crossing Cedar creek with a bold span of ninety-three feet, is perhaps the most celebrated natural curiosity of Virginia. Its height, 215 feet, is greater than that of the Falls of Niagara, and for sublimity, grace and beauty, it is well worthy of being visited by all who appreciate the rarest wonders of nature. It is too well known by description to attempt such repetition here, but no description can prepare the visitor for the revelation of its awe-inspiring and majestic beauty.

ROCKBRIDGE ALUM AND JORDAN ALUM SPRINGS,

eight miles from Goshen, five miles from Millboro', Chesapeake and Ohio Railroad. In the county of Rockbridge, so named from the far famed Natural Bridge, are situated these two adjoining watering-places, to which the point of departure, from the trains, is either Goshen or Millboro'. Stage coaches here, as at the stations of other springs, meet the trains to carry visitors to their destination, over a smooth road and through beautiful mountain scenery.

highly recommended in dyspepsia and affections of the liver and kidneys.

Their proximity to the railroad induces many to select these springs as a resort for the hot season.

ROCKBRIDGE BATHS,

are in Rockbridge county, Va., eleven miles from Goshen. Leaving the railroad at Goshen and taking stages for the "Baths," the traveller passes over a route whose impressions of beauty can never be effaced. The road leads through the "Goshen Pass" and along the bank of North River, both famous for their wild and picturesque scenery, at all times, but especially in Summer, when the mountains are covered from base to top with laurel and ivy in full bloom. Half-way between Goshen and Lexington and on the banks of the river are beautifully located the "Rockbridge Baths," which affords many attractions as a Summer resort for either invalids or pleasure seekers. The hotel, spacious and comfortable, is in a large and shady lawn, and within a few yards of the "bath," the luxury of which can only be appreciated by those who have bathed in its health-restoring crystal waters. The water is very beneficial for all cutaneous diseases and is highly strengthening and invigorating in cases of general debility; rheumatism and affections of the liver also receive much relief from its

The many testimonials of the efficacy of these waters, and the studious care for the comfort, pleasure and satisfaction of guests, annually attract a large number to these "Fountains of Health," which are nestled in a beautiful valley at the base of the North and Mill mountains, and which possess many attractions, commending them alike to the invalid, the seeker of recreation and the votary of pleasure.

THE ROCKBRIDGE ALUM SPRINGS

began to attract attention about the year 1830; persons from the adjacent country were in the habit of visiting them and camping out, sleeping for weeks in their wagons and rude huts, that they might avail themselves of the virtue of these waters in the cure of eruptive and cutaneous diseases. They were found very efficacious in the cure of obstinate and indolent ulcers, many of them of a scrofulous character. In consequence of these successful cures, the reputation of the waters gradually spread, and persons laboring under other diseases were induced to give them a trial. The diseases for which the Rockbridge Spring is now resorted to, are all the scrofulous and cutaneous varieties, chronic dyspepsia, diseases of the glandular system and disordered state of the secretions in general.

"The predominent taste is of alum, which is the largest ingredient of the mixture; but with it are combined iron, lime, magnesia, sodium, soda, ammonia and potash, and the chief solvents are sulphuric and carbonic acids."

The springs, four in number, are basins hollowed out at the base of the ledge of shales lying at the foot of Mill Mountain, and these waters, which are of different degrees of strength, may be administered fresh from the fountains to the patients in various stages of disease. About 350 yards southeast of the hotel, there is also a chalybeate spring, which issues from a hill on the North Mountain side of the valley.

There are accommodation for five or six hundred guests, on the hotel and cottage plan, which seems so popular in the Virginia mountains; nor are the pleasures of this Summer resort neglected, as the means of ministering to gaiety and cheerfulness have been provided on a liberal scale. The mountains around abound with game and the streams with trout.

THE JORDAN ALUM SPRINGS

are but a short distance from and adjacent to the Rockbridge Alum; they have more lately come into public notice, but have attained no small share of popularity for the remedial virtues of their waters and the attractiveness of their grounds as a place of resort during the Summer months. From an analysis of the waters, Prof. Gilliam considers "that they are essentially the same as those of the Rockbridge Alum, and no doubt in the cure of diseases will be found as efficacious."

"The character of the water is *alterative* or *entrophic*, *tonic*, *diuretic*, *astringent* or *purgative*, according to the manner of using them. The diseases to which they are applicable are scrofulous affections, bronchitis, incipient consumption, dyspepsia, diarrhœa and chronic inflammation of the kidneys, bladder and urethra."

The accommodations are all modern, consisting of a "Grand Hotel," containing spacious halls and parlors, the handsomest and largest ball-room in the mountains, well ventilated dining and lodging rooms, lighted with gas, hot and cold baths on every floor; and double cottages near the hotel, which, with the exception of gas, are furnished in every respect like the main-building. The means for amusements are such as are usually provided at the Virginia Springs and in addition, is the delightful drive and visit to the Natural Bridge.

THE MILLBORO' HOUSE,

at Millboro' station, Chesapeake and Ohio Railroad, 176 miles from Richmond. This delightful Summer resort is most eligibly located immediately upon the line of the Chesapeake and Ohio Railroad, at an elevation of 1,700 feet above the level of the sea, in the midst of fine mountain scenery, and within a few hours travel of all the famous watering places in this region. The atmosphere is dry, pure and invigorating, and the nights always cool and refreshing. The mineral waters consist of a chalybeate and a sulphur spring, quite different in their chemical characters; the one of them being allied to the chalybeate and the other to the alkaline sulphur waters, and, accordingly, their medical applications are curative in a great variety of diseases. In the hotel accommodations, sufficient for seventy-five persons, visitors will find the comforts and conveniences of a home.

THE MILLBORO' SPRINGS

are two miles from Millboro' station, on the stage route to the Warm Springs, and near the banks of the Cow Pasture River; and being conveniently accessible by rail and wire communication, while possessing the advantages of pleasant temperature, mountain scenery and sulphur water, have become a favorite Summer retreat especially for the families of such gentlemen of business as are able to spend only a few days at a time from their posts of duty.

The accommodations are comfortable and quiet, and so especially suited for ladies and children wishing to avail themselves of bracing mountain air and mineral water, without the bustle and excitement of the more fashionable watering places.

To the angler and sportsman this place is especially delightful on account of the close proximity of good fishing and hunting grounds.

THE WALLAWHATOOLA SPRINGS,

three miles from Millboro' station and one mile from the Millboro' Springs, is also a quiet and pleasant retreat for families during the hot season, although the accommodations are somewhat limited, being sufficient for 60 guests only. The waters are entirely different from its neighbor, the Millboro' Springs, being very strongly impregnated with *alum* and *iron*, and, by their wonderful success in curing various forms of dyspepsia, have not only a wide and well earned, but a steady increasing reputation.

THE BATH ALUM SPRINGS,

Bath county, Va., ten miles from Millboro', Chesapeake and Ohio Railroad, are situated in an extensive cove near the eastern base of the Warm Spring mountain, on the stage road leading from Millboro' to the Warm Springs, five miles from the latter.

The alum waters issue from a slate cliff and are received into small reservoirs, which differ essentially from each other; one of them being of a very strong chalybeate with but little alum, another of a milder chalybeate with more alum, while the others are alum of different degrees of strength, but all containing an appreciable quantity of iron. Dr. Strother thinks very favorably of them in *scrofulous*, *eruptive* and *dyspeptic affections*.

The improvements here are extensive and convenient, affording comfortable and elegant accommodations for a large company.

DAGGER'S SPRINGS,

Botetourt county, Va., ten miles from Clifton Forge, Chesapeake and Ohio Railroad. This far-famed old watering place is in the vicinity of some of the grandest mountain scenery in the State, and was long known as the Dibbrell Springs. There are few, if any, situated in our mountains where a

period of relaxation from the cares and business of life can be more agreeably spent.

The spring, which arises on a pretty lawn in front of the hotel, is a very bland and agreeable sulphur water, acting as a *diuretic, aperient* and gentle *alterative*. Holding in solution essentially the same medical ingredients that distinguish our best sulphur waters, it may be used advantageously in the various diseases for which sulphur waters generally are employed. It is a valuable dyspeptic water, rarely failing to produce beneficial effects in forms of that disease.

To the sportsman and angler this place has special attractions, for the game and fishing for which it is noted as "the best in the State."

The accommodations are attractive and appropriate. The visitors, in addition to the amusements provided at the Springs, are frequently induced by the pleasant drives and beautiful scenery to visit the Natural Bridge and Peaks of Otter, both of which are within a convenient distance.

THE WARM, HOT AND HEALING SPRINGS,

Bath county, Va. In the beautiful Warm Springs Valley, lying between the Warm Spring mountain and the rugged Alleghany, within a space of eight or ten miles, are situated groups of mineral springs, *among the most celebrated* in the mountains of the Virginias for the unsurpassed beauty and grandeur of their scenery, their delightful, salubrious and invigorating climate, and above all for the remedial and restorative properties of their mineral waters, which in many cases have restored to health and vigor suffering invalids upon whom all the resources of medical skill had been exhausted in vain.

The stage route to the springs is either from Millboro' or Covington on the Chesapeake and Ohio Railroad, and over a turnpike of easy grades. The view in ascending the mountains was thus vividly described by Miss Sedgwick 35 years ago, "We ascended for four miles, winding up a road resembling the ascent of the Catskill, but affording glimpses of far more beautiful mountain scenery. When we reached the summit the grandest scene my eyes ever lit on, save Niagara, was under my eye. An amphitheatre of deep, deep glens below, mountain rising over mountain, one stretching beyond another, some in conical peaks, others in soft, wavy lines and others broken into fantastic shapes, the sunbeams here and there piercing the dark flying clouds and giving to the whole scene the effect of a painter's pencil." On the road from Millboro', in a high ledge, near the bank of the Cow Pasture River, is the mouth of the "Blowing Cave," which is said to have been explored some distance without any other outlet having been found. In intense hot weather the *air comes out* with such force as to prostrate the weeds at the entrance; whilst in cold weather it is as strongly *drawn inward*. On the same stream with the "Blowing Cave" is the "Flowing and Ebbing Spring," from which, at irregular intervals, the water bursts forth with great force and volume. On the road from Covington the traveller passes the riotous cascade of "Falling Spring" and the splendid scenery of Jackson's River.

THE WARM SPRINGS,

fifteen miles from Millboro', twenty-three miles from Covington. These health-giving fountains were the first known and celebrated for their curative virtues. The flow of water from the springs is most abundant. Besides the drinking spring there are two immense baths, one for gentlemen, 120 feet, and the other for ladies, 150 feet in circumference, which are estimated to receive 6,000 gallons per minute, and from which the outflow forms a stream sufficient to drive a large mill. "Their temperature is 98°, and as a pleasure bath there is none superior."

"These waters are diuretic, diaphoretic, gentle purgative and alterative in their influence, when taken internally; and by these conjoint agencies act efficiently in stimulating obstructed glands and removing from the system vitiated secretions and morbid products. Locally applied, they are gently relaxant, stimulant and sorbefacient, hence admirably adapted to the treatment and

FALLING SPRING FALLS.

cure of the following numerous class of diseased conditions, viz: Chronic gout and rheumatism, torpidity of the liver, with attendant consequences, as indigestion, constipation, dropsical effusion, &c., paralysis in its various forms, enlargements of the spleen, chronic swellings of the joints, chronic diarrhœa, resulting either from debility or torpid liver, some forms of neuralgia, dyspepsia, together with the large class of female diseases, resulting from engorgement and enlargement of the uterus."

The climate is delicious, the thermometer seldom rising higher than 85° in the hottest days; and the nights are always cool and refreshing.

The accommodations are sufficient for a very large company, consisting of a spacious

THE HEALING SPRINGS.

main-building and cottages. The attractions are well calculated to cause one "to take no note of time, but from its loss." Besides the local amusements are the interchange of visits with friends at the other Springs in the vicinity, and, for the sportsman and angler, abundant game and fish within convenient distance.

THE HOT SPRINGS,

twenty miles from Millboro', eighteen miles from Covington. In the Warm Spring Valley, at the head of an intersecting secondary valley, are situated the Hot Springs, five miles from the Warm and three miles from the Healing Springs, and the hotel is so situated as to command a noble view in both directions and catch the Summer breeze from every quarter.

Within the grounds are found, in close proximity, numerous bold springs of hot and cold mineral water, ranging in temperature from 50 to 110 degrees Fahrenheit. In their extraordinary remedial powers in many of the most serious, painful and dangerous chronic diseases that afflict the human race, this watering place offers to invalids, suffering from the maladies for which thermal waters are recommended, advantages and facilities for the recovery of health which are not surpassed, or perhaps not equalled, at any of those celebrated thermal springs in France and Germany, that for many centuries have been places of great resort for persons in search of health.

"The drinking waters comprise a great variety and include *sulphur, magnesia* and *ferruginous alum* waters, and the baths are the most complete and extensive in the United States, consisting of invalid baths, boiler baths, sulphur baths, hot spout baths, mud bath, octagon bath, warm baths, the ladies' pleasure bath, supplied from the new 'Schlagenbad' spring, which, resembling in temperature and hygienic effect the German Spa of that name, is in high favor with the ladies, and the gentlemen's pleasure bath, which is supplied from a very bold *magnesian* spring at a temperature of 78°, and is of such extent as to constitute a large swimming bath." The accommodations and attractions are equal to any watering place in the mountains.

THE HEALING SPRINGS,

fifteen miles from Covington; twenty-three miles from Millboro'. The scenery is wild, grand and picturesque, and the climate delightful—the mercury rarely rising above 80° usually 60° to 75°.

The supply of water is abundant, being derived from four springs of essentially the same character, each of which affords a large volume of water. The water is beautifully bright and crystaline, and the ever-bursting bubbles of gas that escape with the water and float in myriads of vesicles upon its surface impart to it a peculiar, sparkling appearance. Its temperature is uniformly 85° and 88° Fahrenheit.

The bathing accommodations are so extensive as to be able to furnish *hot* baths and those of the natural temperature, as the necessities demand.

A lady says: "Among the many virtues possessed by the Healing waters, there is one that should not be held too lightly (especially by the fair sex), viz: the rare power it has in softening and beautifying the skin, by bathing in it. It produces the most delightful satin-like feeling, and renders the complexion peculiarly clear and transparent; gives to the the cheek a new tint, and makes one fancy the wrinkles are smoothed away.

The waters of these Springs are almost identical in their chemical analysis to the famous Schlagenbad and Ems in Germany.

Another peculiarity of this water is its generation of a fine silken-looking moss, which is much celebrated as an application to certain forms of opthalmia, and to old and irritable ulcers. It has also been used with benefit in certain forms of eczema and other diseases of the skin, attended with inflammatory irritation."

The waters of the Healing Springs are eminently beneficial in all diseases of the skin and mucous membranes, and especially in those cases arising from an impure state of the blood, such as rheumatism, dyspepsia, chronic diarrhœa, dysentery and many others.

The accommodations are extensive, consisting of main-building and 40 cottages within convenient distance.

The attractions usually offered at watering places are provided; hunting and fishing entertain the sportsman and angler.

THE SWEET, AND SWEET CHALYBEATE SPRINGS.

Leaving the Chesapeake and Ohio trains at Alleghany station, 222 miles from Richmond, and taking the stage-coaches, which run regularly during the Springs season in connection with the trains, the traveller has a pleasant drive over a good turnpike, and "comes upon the clear waters of a little creek rushing over a rocky cleft, at 'Beaver Dam,' with a noise and pother far exceeding that of the famous cascade of Lodore, and with such a picturesqueness of dark green in the foliage, and brilliant refractions and reflections of broken sunlight in the descending drops, that were 'Beaver Dam' in the Adirondacks we should have had pictures of it by the score. The falls derives its name from the fact that here the beavers built a barrier across the stream, of which the net work may still be seen in petrifaction."

Nine miles from the station, and just within the border of Alleghany county, Va., are the Sweet Chalybeate (Red Sweet), and one mile beyond, in Monroe county, W. Va., are the Sweet (Old Sweet) Springs, in a charming valley bounded by the lofty Alleghany and Sweet Spring mountains.

THE SWEET SPRINGS,

Monroe county, West Va., ten miles from Alleghany. Few mineral waters have ac-

BEAVER DAM FALLS.

quired such extended and well merited celebrity as the Sweet Springs; the chief distinguishing feature of the water is the predominance of the carbonic acid which it contains. In varieties of dyspepsia, in scrofulous habits from enlargement of the bronchial glands; to females who have become enervated by long confinement or have suffered for want of exercise and fresh air, in sub-acute rheumatism and in neuralgia attacks, the Sweet Spring waters internally and externally employed are eminently useful. The temperature of the water is 73°, and the spring rises in a large cylindrical reservoir, from opposite sides of which it flows to the baths, one for ladies and the other for gentlemen, each about 60 x 30 feet. Contiguous to the spring is a grove of a few old natives of the forest, that have fortunately escaped the axe of the spoiler. The buildings are eminently comfortable, and the grounds are beautiful and extensive.

Deer and other game abound in the immediate neighborhood, and facilities for hunting and fishing are exceptionally good. All means of local amusements provided at other watering places may be found here.

THE SWEET CHALYBEATE SPRINGS,

Alleghany county, Va., nine miles from Alleghany. These Springs greatly resemble the Sweet, and were known in their early history as the "Red Sweet." There are two medicinal springs essentially the same,

WHITE SULPHUR SPRINGS.

The most famous of all these "Fountains of Health" is

THE WHITE SULPHUR SPRINGS,

Greenbrier Co., W. Va., immediately on Chesapeake and Ohio Railroad, 227 miles from Richmond, Va., 194 miles from Huntington, W. Va.

These are the Springs *par excellence* of the wonderful Springs Region—the resort of the gay and fashionable—the place where pleasure seeking reigns supreme. The situation is elevated, 2,000 feet above tide-water, and is beautifully picturesque, surrounded by mountains on every side. The grounds are in a basin, near the centre of which is located the main-building, said to be the largest in the South; it is 400 feet in length with a corresponding width, and covering more than an acre of ground; containing receiving rooms, dining-room, ball-room, parlor, &c. The parlor is very spacious and the dining-room is "one of the largest in the world," being upwards of 300 feet long and proportionally wide, conveniently seating 1,200 persons. In addition to the main-building there are a large number of small cottages built on the rise of the ground bordering the basin, and within convenient distance of the hotel. The grounds, some portion of which are heavily wooded, are artistically laid out with wide and nicely gravelled avenues, which lead one into all sorts of romantic places and romantic situations. As a writer in *Scribner's Magazine* truly remarks: There is a singular, and for a fashionable watering place, an extraordinary look of comfort and careless ease about the White Sulphur. These Spring are the popular resort, not only of young people, but as well of stern warriors, eloquent orators, profound statemen and distinguished men and women generally of the State and nation; and here in congenial society all find relaxation from

except that the "Red Spring" contains much more iron than the other. The water of the "Red Spring," issuing from beneath heavy limestone arches, is the characteristic water of the place, and most relied upon for drinking and bathing; it is the outflow of three fountains separated by natural stone partitions, but all running into one common sluice; one of them being very much bolder and also very much colder than the others. The flow of water is 800 gallons per minute. The great charm of the place is the enclosed *pools*, for *plunge bathing*, which are pleasant, invigorating and health-bestowing, and as the sparkling waters flow fresh from the springs, these pools afford in perfection the true luxury of bathing. The temperature of the water as it flows from the three different heads is from 75° to 79°, varying slightly at different times, but never exceeding one or two degrees of variation. The waters of these Springs used internally and externally are beneficial for numerous *diseases* of *females*, for *cholera infantum*, obstinate cases of *intermittent fever* when medicines seem to have lost their efficacy, for jaundice, neuralgia, gout and rheumatism, and for chronic diarrhœa and dysentery.

Delightful drives materially aid the quietly disposed guests to pass their time pleasantly, while the sportsman and angler rejoice in the abundant game and fish for which this region is noted.

business, and inducements to pleasant occupation, whilst the bracing, invigorating atmosphere serves as an invaluable tonic to the physical system. The attractions here are various in kind and degree; in addition to views of wild and picturesque mountain scenery, pleasant walks and beautiful rides and drives, there are masquerade and fancy balls throughout the season, billiard-tables, bowling-alleys, pistol-gallery, and band-music for lawn and ball-room.

There is a neat little chapel on the grounds, which is always well attended, and where services are held by ministers of all denominations.

During the Summer the thermometer ranges between 55° and 65° Fahrenheit, and rarely attains a greater height than 80° at any time of the day; and the temperature of the waters is 62°, from which they do not vary. The spring yields 30 gallons per minute, never being affected either by rain or dry weather, and the distinctive medical influences of the water upon the system are *cathartic, diuretic, sudorific* and *alterative*. In chronic affections these waters are peculiarly curative; various diseases of the stomach, liver, spleen, kidneys and bladder, and some derangements of the brain and nervous system are treated successfully with them, as well as various affections of the skin, chronic affections of the bowels, gout, rheumatism and many others.

THE CALWELL HOUSE.

Immediately adjacent to the White Sulphur Springs, and within half a mile of the railroad station, is situated this long established and favorite Summer retreat. In addition to the magnificent surroundings and health giving fountain of the White Sulphur Springs, many other varieties of mineral waters are on or adjacent to the grounds of the Calwell House, and at a short distance is a magnificent bath-house, containing two bath-rooms, each 30 x 60 feet, with an unvarying temperature of 62°. The streams feeding these baths exhibit a marked affinity to the waters of the famous Hot Springs of Arkansas, and the water is considered a specific in rheumatic and kindred ailments. A Chalybeate Spring, contiguous to the bath, is claimed to be the strongest in the mountains, and adds to the attractions of a visit. The hotel buildings are spacious, comprising reception-rooms and parlors, and broad shaded piazzas affording, regardless of weather, the most delightful promenades and views; verdant lawns, shaded lanes and cozy dells

entice even the invalid to exercise. The beautiful Howard's Creek, fed by innumerable mineral fountains and affording convenient and refreshing plunge baths, flows within a hundred yards of the hotel. A spacious ball-room, a well shaded, level croquet ground and romantic drives challenge the attention of the visitor.

THE RED SULPHUR SPRINGS,

Monroe county, Va., 14 miles from Lowell, Chesapeake and Ohio Railroad. For more than forty years the Red Sulphur has drawn to its fountains, in the heart of the Virginia mountain fastnesses, many victims of disease, but until lately the rugged barriers deterred the pleasure seeking public from enjoying the unrivalled grandeur of its approaches. Now, however, the Chesapeake and Ohio Railway, and a fine turnpike from Lowell station, enable one to visit with comfort this Spring, of which Dr. Henry Huntt says— "It is not excelled by any place of resort among the salubrious mountains of the Old Dominion, either in magnificence of scenery, beauty, taste, comfort or health." "The approach is beautifully romantic and picturesque; wending his way around a high mountain, the traveller is charmed by the sudden view of his resting place, some hundreds of feet immediately beneath him, into which he descends to a verdant glen surrounded on all sides by lofty mountains." Another writer says—"In the middle of this valley, on a lawn studded with noble trees, and sheltered by circling mountains that look down from a thousand feet, rise the mysterious fountains of the Red Sulphur Springs. Here in a basin some ten feet below the level of the surrounding lawn, are two springs bubbling from neat marble cisterns, and discharging their surplus volume, through pipes, into the neighboring brook. The visitor descends to the precious fluid by an approach of several steps, and stands in the shelter of a noble pavilion in the form of a Grecian temple erected over the spot." "The Red Sulphur water is already a well established specific for all forms of *Pulmonary disease,* and is fast becoming the Mecca of consumptives." "Around mineral springs, as a general rule, the country people refuse belief in their virtues; not so with the Red Sulphur Springs. The virtues of these Springs find their most enthusiastic heralds in the country around them. Diseases of the bronchial as well as those of the secretive tissues here also find relief; but the Red Sulphur water may be emphatically proclaimed the *king of consumption.''*

KANAWHA FALLS,

333 miles from Richmond, just beyond the junction of the New and Gauley Rivers, which, uniting, form the Kanawha, is the favorite destination for excursionists from the White Sulphur and other springs, and is also a noted fishing station for parties from Cincinnati and other Western cities. The accommodations are pleasant and ample—not only a large hotel immediately on the line of the road at this point, but on the opposite side of the river the old ''Stockton'' House, which was the famous stopping place for travellers, in the days of stages, before the railroad was constructed. On the route from the Virginia Springs, at the crossing of New River and nine miles before reaching the Kanawha Falls, are the celebrated ''Hawk's Nest'' and ''Lover's Leap,'' the former a bold, perpendicular cliff towering many hundred feet above the river and the latter, about the same altitude, an immense rectangular block of sandstone jutting out over the original forest trees far below. Between Hawk's Nest and Kanawha Falls the traveller passes the wonderful gorge, or canon, of New River, bounded by rugged and massive walls of rock on both sides, through which, and midway along the face of the cliffs, now on benches, now through tunnels and now over immense masses of gnarled and shattered rock, smoothly and safely with gentlest curves and lightest grades the Chesapeake and Ohio Railroad finds its way.

THE OLDEN-TIME MODE OF CONVEYANCE.

—THE—
PIEDMONT AIR-LINE,
—VIA—
Charlotte, Danville and Richmond,
IS THE
SHORTEST & MOST COMFORTABLE ROUTE
BETWEEN
THE SOUTHERN STATES AND THE VIRGINIA SPRINGS,
AND BETWEEN
New Orleans, Mobile, Montgomery, Atlanta, Savannah, Augusta,
COLUMBIA AND NEW YORK.

EQUIPMENT FIRST-CLASS IN ALL ITS APPOINTMENTS.

Passenger Trains equipped with the Westinghouse Automatic Air-brake
and all modern improvements and Appliances conducive to
the Safety and Comfort of the Travelling Public.

This Route passes through a section of country noted for its

SALUBRIOUS CLIMATE, GRAND AND VARIED SCENERY,
THRIVING AND ATTRACTIVE CITIES AND TOWNS,

And makes close connection at Richmond, Va., with the Chesapeake and Ohio Railway for
the various Springs and Mountain Resorts.

ROUND-TRIP TICKETS
TO ALL THE
VIRGINIA SPRINGS & WATERING PLACES
WILL BE ON SALE DURING THE SEASON,
JUNE 1ST, TO OCTOBER 31ST,

At all the principal Ticket Offices in the South.   For arrival and departure of trains see
Time Cards and apply to your nearest Railroad Agent.

J. L. WALDROP,	**J. R. MACMURDO,**
Gen'l Southern Agent.	*Gen'l Passenger Agent.*

ATLANTC COAST LINE,
FAST MAIL PASSENGER ROUTE,
—VIA—
WILMINGTON, N. C. AND RICHMOND, VA.

DOUBLE DAILY TRAINS.

Quick Time and Sure Connections.

Note the Through Car Schedule, unequalled by any other Line

BETWEEN THE EAST AND THE SOUTH.

PULLMAN PALACE SLEEPING CARS DAILY (EXCEPT SUNDAY) BETWEEN JACKSONVILLE, FLA., AND WILMINGTON, N. C., AND DAILY BETWEEN SAVANNAH, GA., AND WILMINGTON.

PULLMAN PALACE SLEEPING CARS BETWEEN CHARLESTON, S. C., AND WILMINGTON (DAILY).

PULLMAN PALACE SLEEPING CARS BETWEEN SAVANNAH, GA., AND WASHINGTON, D. C., (DAILY EXCEPT SUNDAY.)

PULLMAN PALACE SLEEPING CARS BETWEEN SAVANNAH, GA., AND BOSTON, MASS., (SEMI–WEEKLY.)

LUCAS SLEEPING CARS BETWEEN AUGUSTA, GA., AND WILMINGTON, N. C.

ATLANTIC COAST LINE PARLOR CARS BETWEEN WILMINGTON AND RICHMOND.

RATES AS LOW AS ANY OTHER LINE.

BAGGAGE CHECKED AND THROUGH TICKETS SOLD

TO AND FROM ALL

PRINCIPAL POINTS NORTH, EAST AND SOUTH.

A. POPE,
Gen. Pass. Agent.

WILMINGTON, N. C., April 1st, 1878.

46

JAMES RIVER

—BY—

DAY-LIGHT!

HISTORICAL SCENERY!

DREWRY'S BLUFF—Fort Darling.

AIKEN'S LANDING—Exchange of Prisoners.

DUTCH GAP CANAL—Butler's

BERMUDA HUNDREDS—Butler bottled.

CITY POINT—Grant's Base.

Harrison's Landing--McClellan's Retreat

JAMESTOWN:

FIRST ENGLISH SETTLEMENT IN AMERICA.

FORTRESS MONROE--Largest in America,

OLD POINT, HYGEIA HOTEL, RIP-RAPS,

NORFOLK, &c., &c., &c.

SPLENDID STEAMERS, QUICK TIME,

SEA BREEZES, ELEGANT FARE.

Straight and Round Trip Excursion Tickets, over this beautiful Route, on sale at all principal offices of Chesapeake and Ohio Railroad to

OLD POINT & NORFOLK,

And at Norfolk and on steamers to the Virginia Springs and Western Points, via Chesapeake and Ohio Railroad.

Richmond, Va.   L. B. TATUM, Supt.

Virginia Steamboat Line.

—GENERAL—

RAILROAD TICKET OFFICE.

Richmond Transfer & Baggage Express Company,

826 MAIN STREET.

We sell RAILROAD and STEAMBOAT TICKETS to all points reached by any lines leading from Richmond. Rates always same as at depots.

We have on sale a full line of SUMMER EXCURSION TICKETS via all Railroad and Steamboat lines leading from Richmond, and via the Pennsylvania Railroad, embracing all WATERING PLACES, LAKES, SEASIDE and MOUNTAIN RESORTS in America and Canada.

We are agents for the CUNARD, WHITE STAR, NATIONAL and ALLEN LINE of foreign steamers. We are prepared to furnish passage and state room accommodations on either of the above lines always on same terms that they can be procured from the general offices of either of the lines.

We call for and check baggage from hotels and private residences in all parts of the city to all points in the United States. Baggage rates 25 cents for each piece. No extra charges for carrying baggage up or down stairs. Special rates for large lots of baggage.

We call for passengers in any part of the city for any trains or steamers leaving the city. Rates, 50 cents for single passenger; $1.50 for four passengers from one point. Escort carried to depot or steamer free of charge. Also, pleasure carriages at reasonable rates by the hour. Special rates for marriage parties and funerals.

We have an agent on all trains arriving in the city, who will take up checks and deliver baggage, or from whom carriages may be procured for passengers on arrival at depot.

All orders for carriages or baggage calls should be left at office,

826 MAIN STREET,

During the week, and at Stables, cor. Ninth and Cary sts., on Sunday.

OFFICE HOURS: 7 A. M. to 9 P. M.

A. W. GARBER, Proprietor.

A TELEGRAPH OFFICE HAS BEEN OPENED AT OUR OFFICE, AND MES-SAGES ARE SENT TO ALL POINTS.

GREENBRIER WHITE SULPHUR SPRINGS,

WEST VIRGINIA.

So long and favorably known for their valuable ALTERATIVE WATERS, their charming Summer climate, and the large and fashionable crowds that annually resort to them, will be opened on 1st June.

RATES OF CHARGES FOR SEASON OF 1878, VIZ:

BOARD, $3.00 PER DAY;

$20.00 PER WEEK;

$75.00 PER MONTH, OF THIRTY DAYS.

☞ Special arrangements may be made for large families that spend the entire season here.

☞ Special Rates will also be made for September and October.

☞ Children and Colored Servants half price. White Servants in proportion to the accommodations furnished.

☞ A First-class Band will be in attendance to enliven the Lawns and Ball Room.

☞ Masquerade and Fancy Balls occasionally through the season.

☞ Telegraphic line in operation to the Springs.

☞ A LIVERY is kept for the accommodation of visitors.

☞ A well organized LAUNDRY, where all washing for the guests will be neatly done at low rates—and to protect ourselves and our guests from loss and outside intrusion, we must insist that the washing of visitors be confined to our laundry, for the proper management of which we are always responsible.

☞ The Lessees wish it to be distinctly understood that the use of the White Sulphur Water, Baths and Grounds will be strictly confined to those who are the guests of this establishment, and that their use will be withheld from all others, except upon their paying $2 per day for such use. Permanent residents of the county alone excepted.

PHYSICIANS TO THE SPRINGS.

Prof. J. J. Moorman, M. D.   -   -   T. B. Fuqua, M. D.

GEO. L PEYTON & CO.,
Proprietors.

Maj. B. F. EAKLE, Chief Clerk.

THE CALWELL HOUSE

Greenbrier County, West Virginia,

ADJOINING WHITE SULPHUR SPRINGS.

This long established and favorite Summer Retreat having recently changed ownership, the present proprietor, with the accessories at his command for the comfort of guests, feels justified in assuring those visiting the Mountains, either for health or recreation, that his establishment shall continue worthy of the reputation it now enjoys.

THE MOUNTAIN WATERS.

Mineral Springs of many varieties, and all health inducing, are on and adjacent to the grounds.

THE HOTEL.

The spacious hotel buildings have large, well-furnished reception, dining-parlors and bed-rooms, broad, shaded piazzas, aggregating 550 feet in length, affording at all seasons, without regard to weather, the most delightful of promenades and views.

THE COMMISSARIAT.

Apart from the luxuries of the local and eastern markets, the forests and streams of this noted game region will be made tributary to the table d'Hote. A restaurant of rare excellence, in charge of the famous *Chef de cuisine*, Zetelle, is attached to the ladies' and gentlemen's dining-parlors, where breakfasts, dinners and suppers will be served to parties at any hour—game being now, as ever, a prominent feature in the *menu*. An attentive hostess will see that ladies have all their wants supplied, and every energy of the proprietor, assisted by trained and obliging attendants, will be enlisted in making guests feel at home.

MEANS FOR SOCIAL ENJOYMENT.

The votaries of Terpsichore will possess in the hotel a spacious ball-room, open at all times, while a well-shaded, level croquet ground will challenge the attention of the ladies.

LIVERY ADVANTAGES.

Ample stable accommodations for horses and vehicles, with skilled hostlers, familiar with the Mountains, will always be supplied.

ROOMS, &c.,

Rooms can be secured by letter or telegraph. All inquiries promptly and truthfully answered.

OPEN ALL THE YEAR.

The Calwell House will be kept open throughout the year, with no diminution in service or appointment—the proprietor giving to his guests, especially those from malarial districts, a fixed home at the most delightful season in the mountains, when other summer resorts are closed. They may be assured that extra charges will be the exception, and not the rule, at this Hotel.

The RATES OF CHARGES for the Season of 1878, are as follows:

BOARD, $2 50 per day; $15 00 per week; $50 per month of 30 days.

Inducements will be offered to large families who spend the entire season. For September and October reductions will be made. Children and colored servants, half price. The LAUNDRY is in charge of those most capable of rendering satisfaction. For further particulars, address

J. H. OREY CARY, Proprietor,

Calwell House, White Sulphur Springs, Greenbrier Co., W. Va.

50

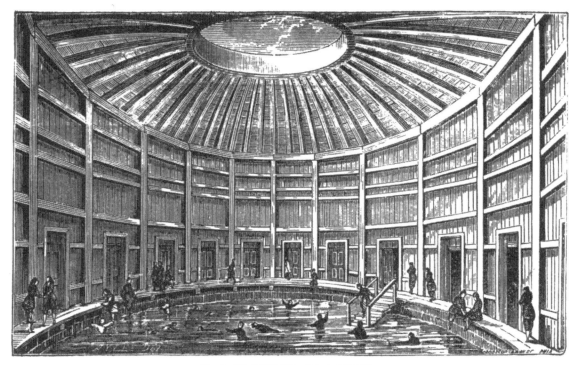

LADIES' BATH,
WARM SPRINGS, BATH COUNTY, VIRGINIA,

50 feet in Diameter. Warm Sulphur Water, 98° temperature.

THE WARM SPRINGS,

ARE NOW OPEN, AND WILL BE

Kept open until the 15th of October.

The above is a correct view of the Ladies' Bath. The Gentlemen's Bath is a similar one, only not quite so large. There is a flow of SIX THOUSAND gallons of Warm Sulphur Water per minute.

The BATHS are said to be the FINEST IN THE WORLD.

The internal use of the water, conjoined with the Baths, has been found signally beneficial in the following diseases :

CHRONIC AND SUB ACUTE RHEUMATISM AND GOUT,

NEURALGIA, PARALYSIS, DYSPEPSIA,

(especially that form connected with disturbance of the Liver or a Torpid state of the Bowels),

DISORDERS OF THE URINARY ORGANS,

CHRONIC DISEASES OF THE SKIN,

ALL DISEASES OF THE BLOOD,

AND THE DISEASES PECULIAR TO FEMALES.

PASSENGERS FOR THE WARM SPRINGS GET OFF AT MILLBORO' DEPOT.

Apply to the proprietor of hotel at that place for transportation. He will furnish comfortable carriages and baggage wagons at moderate prices. Stage coupons received.

May 1st, 1878.   JNO. L. EUBANK, *Proprietor.*

SEND FOR PAMPHLETS.

GET OFF AT COVINGTON

—for the—

HEALING SPRINGS,

BATH COUNTY, VA.

THESE SPRINGS, LONG AND FAVORABLY KNOWN TO THE PUBLIC,

——will be——

OPENED FOR THE RECEPTION OF VISITORS JUNE 1, 1878.

The accommodations are equal to any in the mountain.

TERMS: Per day, $3.00; per week, $17.50; per month, from $40 to $50, according to number of persons, and rooms required, and length of time they remain. Children under ten years and colored servants, half price. White servants according to accommodations required.

To THE INVALID this is the most desirable route, as the Turnpike to the Springs is the FINEST MOUNTAIN ROAD IN THE STATE.

THE TOURIST will find the scenery along the route equal to any in the country, passing for several miles along the Valley of Jackson River, in FULL VIEW OF THE CELEBRATED FALLING SPRINGS. A view of these Falls is worth a trip over this route.

THE HEALING SPRINGS are situated in the Beautiful Valley of the Warm Springs Mountains, and are 1,500 feet above tide-water. The air is pure, dry and bracing. Fogs, so common to most of the mountain resorts, are almost unknown here. They are centrally located with reference to the other Springs. A circuit of fifty miles will embrace all the Springs in the Spring region of Virginia and West Virginia.

The main buildings, three in number, are of brick, surrounded by forty beautiful cottages, capable of rooming three hundred guests. The BALL-ROOM and DINING-ROOM are ample for the entire company. Telegraph and Postoffice in Hotel. GOOD LIVERY attached to the Hotel. MUSIC for Ballroom and lawn.

WM. B. BISHOP,
Proprietor.

STAGES AND OTHER VEHICLES FOR THE SPRINGS LEAVE COVINGTON EVERY MORNING.

Sweet Chalybeate Springs,

KNOWN ALSO AS THE

RED SWEET SPRINGS.

ALLEGHANY COUNTY, VA.,

8 Miles from Alleghany Station, Chesapeake and Ohio Railroad.

These celebrated Springs, so long and favorably known for their valuable Nervine, Tonic and Alterative waters, both as a beverage and bath, will be open for the reception of visitors

JUNE 1, 1878.

Most Luxurious Tonic Baths in America.

GENTLEMEN'S PLUNGE BATHS, LADIES' PLUNGE BATHS,

Also a new and conveniently arranged Bathing establishment. These Baths are supplied by the mineral waters of the Spring, and by means of steam are heated in zinc troughs to any degree of temperature the bather may desire. There are here three fountains, all separated by naturally formed stone partitions, but all running in one common sluice. The water issuing from these is *eight hundred gallons* per minute.

TERMS—Prices to suit the Times.

Board, per Day, - - -		$2 50.
" " Week, - -		$15 00.
" " Month of 30 days,		$35 to $45.

Children under ten years and colored servants, half price.
White servants, according to accommodations.

TELEGRAPH, EXPRESS and POST OFFICE in hotel.

GOOD BILLIARD TABLES. FINE LIVERY,

BOWLING ALLEYS FREE TO VISITORS.

GOOD TROUT FISHING,

DEER AND PHEASANT HUNTING in Season.

Professor Voelker's Brass and String Band will enliven the Lawns and Ball-Rooms.
Pamphlets, giving analyses of the waters, full description of the Springs and containing testimonials from visitors who have been benefitted and cured by the waters, and also embodying certificates from well-known and eminent physicians, to be had on application to the proprietor at the Springs. See also descriptive notice of *these Springs contained in this book.*

Dr. J. E. CHANCELLOR,

Late of University of Va., Resident Physician.

J. B. TINSLEY, Jr.,

Proprietor.

54

SWEET SPRINGS,

Monroe County, West Virginia.

THIS OLD & POPULAR ESTABLISHMENT

will be open

FOR THE ACCOMMODATION OF VISITORS

—on the—

15TH OF JUNE.

No establishment of the kind is its

SUPERIOR IN APPOINTMENTS AND ACCOMMODATION.

All the material used is

FIRST-CLASS IN EVERY DEPARTMENT,

and no pains will be spared to make the guests comfortable in every respect.

A FIRST-CLASS BAND OF MUSIC HAS BEEN ENGAGED FOR THE LAWN AND BALL-ROOM.

MAILS DAILY,

TELEGRAPH OFFICE IN THE HOTEL,

MESSAGES SENT TO ALL PARTS OF THE WORLD,

BILLIARD-TABLES AND BOWLING-ALLEYS FREE OF CHARGE,

A first-class LIVERY, under charge of the hotel, and a STEAM LAUNDRY, where washing will be down in the very best style, at reasonable charges.

Excursion tickets at reduced rates, good for the season, can be obtained at all the railroad offices in the cities.

Alleghany station, on the Chesapeake and Ohio Railroad, is the point of debarcation for the Sweet Springs, where fine four horse coaches will be found in waiting on the arrival of all trains to convey passengers to the Springs, distance 10½ miles.

I. W. YOUNGER,

Superintendent

Jordan Alum Springs,

ROCKBRIDGE COUNTY, VA.

FIVE MILES FROM MILLBORO',

EIGHT MILES FROM GOSHEN,

ON THE CHESAPEAKE & OHIO R. R.

THIS POPULAR PLACE OF RESORT

WILL BE OPEN

For the Reception of Guests

JUNE 1, 1878,

UNDER THE SAME MANAGEMENT WHICH MADE IT SO

ATTRACTIVE to the HEALTH & PLEASURE SEEKING PUBLIC

DURING THE LAST SEASON.

THE COMPLETE APPOINTMENTS OF THE

HOTELS AND COTTAGES

And the many natural advantages of the place present

ATTRACTIONS UNSURPASSED

BY ANY VIRGINIA WATERING PLACE.

RATES.

Per Month,	–	–	$40 to $60, according to location.
Per Week,		–	$20.
Per Day,	–	-	$ 3.

COMFORTABLE STAGES AND CARRIAGES MEET ALL TRAINS arriving at Goshen and Millboro', and Passengers and their baggage will receive prompt attention from polite agents and careful drivers.

J. N. WOODWARD,
MANAGER.

JNO. W. CAMERON.
AGENT.

56

ROCKBRIDGE ALUM SPRINGS, VA.
(OPEN JUNE 1ST.)

JAMES A. FRAZIER, Owner and Proprietor.

Mr. W. A. LEWIS, Cashier; Prof. J. S. DAVIS, (of University of Virginia) Resident Physician; Mr. J. R. CHRISTIAN, Caterer.

READ WHAT THE "MEDICAL SAVANS" SAY OF THE CELEBRATED WATERS.

DR. NOEL, *late Resident Physician*—"I regret at this time I cannot give the profession and the public the results of two years' close attention, for I have given more than ordinary attention to this subject; as two years ago, an invalid and consumptive, so pronounced by six physicians of Baltimore, I sought these springs as a *dernier resort*, and returned in four months a convalescent. I have, therefore, good cause to study well the action of the waters.

CONSUMPTION—I have seen it arrested in its first stage. I have seen softening of the tubercles arrested. I have seen the Consecutive Bronchitis arrested. I have seen patients gain in flesh and health.

BRONCHITIS—Catarrhal—Suppurative—and Rheumatic Bronchitis I have seen cured, and cured permanently.

SCROFULA—Glandular Enlargements, Scrofulous Ulcers, Scrofulous Eruptions, Scrofulous Discharges from Ears and Eyes, &c., I have seen yield most rapidly, and permanent cures result.

CERTIFICATES.

There are many persons who have neither time nor the inclination to read the certificates contained in the pamphlets of the different springs; and, in fact, to such an extent has this practice of giving certificates been carried, that, between advertising quacks and venders of patent medicines, the daily prints are filled *ad nauseum*.

As thoughtful men, we cannot, therefore, ask any community to trust us upon our certificates alone, but we do ask to be trusted upon the certificates and letters of the following erudite and accomplished members of the medical profession.

DR. JAMES L. CABELL, Prof. in the Med. Department, Univ. of Va.; DR. T. GAILLARD THOMAS, Prof. of Obstetrics, College of Physicians and Surgeons, New York.; DR. THOMAS ADDIS EMMET, Surgeon in charge Woman's State Hospital, New York.; DR. M. M. PALLEM, Professor of Obstetrics, St. Louis Medical College; DR. THOMAS L. MADDEN, Professor of the Institute of Medicine, Nashville Medical College.

And letters from such old and experienced men as Dr. Samuel A. Cartright, New Orleans, La., Dr. J. J. Clark, of St. Louis, Mo., and Dr. Wilson, of Baltimore, Md.

DR. CARTRIGHT.—"In truth I know of no waters in Europe or America so rich in medical substances as that of the Rockbridge Springs."

DR. CABELL.—"It is indeed admitted that a more or less considerable proportion of cases of inveterate chronic diseases, for which relief is sought by the use of that water, derive no permanent benefits from it, but it is undeniable that an unusually large proportion of grave and obstinate cases, which baffle the ordinary resources of the healing art, are annually cured at your springs."

DR. THOMAS.—"I would state that I regard it as one of the most efficient astringent and tonic Mineral Waters which I have ever employed."

DR. EMMET.—"I know of no Mineral Waters so efficacious." * * * * * "I have used both the water and dried preparation, or salts, in private practice, and in the woman's Hospital- for several years, to my great satisfaction.

DR. MADDEN.—"The investigation I have given the watering places *in this and other countries*, leads me to the conclusion that *none* have claims superior to the Rockbridge Alum Springs, Va.

DR. MOORMAN, author of the well know work on the Virginia Springs:—"It is a matter of no little importance that the public should be fully apprised of the remarkable influence exerted by the Rockbridge Alum Waters, in strumous diseases especially. *They* have long stood as a reproach to our profession, and never but in these waters has a remedy been found that deserves the name of a *specific* for their cure."

DR. WILSON, of Baltimore says: "I am in the habit of sending more patients to the Rockbridge Alum Springs than anywhere else."

REV. W. S. PLUMER, D. D. the great Southern Divine, says: "The remarkable efficacy of these waters in a large number of diseases is truly wonderful."

The REV. CORNELIUS TYREE, of Virginia, who has been a constant visitor of these Springs for more than thirty years, writes: "Their effect in purifying the blood, in regulating the liver, in giving tone to the stomach, promoting its proper secretions, strengthening its impaired digestion, and in giving general vigor to feeble systems is wonderful; moreover, the cures these waters achieve are mostly radical and permanent."

That great and good man, the REV. JAMES W. ALEXANDER, D. D., New York, writes: "These waters are not a nostrum: everybody sees and knows all about them. They are not a *quack medicine*; the regular faculty exhibit them with due guards and cautions."

The following is from the pen of one of Virginia's purest and ablest editors, JAS. A. COWARDIN, Sr., of the *Dispatch*, and speaks volumes: "It has gained renown more rapidly than any known water, and is always visited by the invalid with a hope that equals faith. Few springs have done so much for the good of men within twenty years as the Rockbridge Alum. * * * * The throng at the Rockbridge Alum always shows that it is 'gay and festive.' They are always sure of a bright season, while the invalid enters the grounds with the confident air of one who had 'come to get well.'"

☞ POST-OFFICE AS ABOVE. SEND FOR PAMPHLETS. ☜

DAGGER'S
White Sulphur Springs,

(FORMERLY DIBBRILL'S.)

BOTETOURT COUNTY, VIRGINIA.

Approached from Clifton Forge on the Chesapeake and Ohio Rail Road, a Station 55 Miles West of Staunton, and 35 Miles East of the Greenbrier White Sulphur Springs.

THIS attractive watering place, having recently changed ownership, has undergone such alterations and repairs, as render it one of the most desirable of the Virginia summer resorts.

All the furniture, bedding and table appointments were purchased, new, in Baltimore last season.

Room department will be under the management of Captain GEORGE E. TAYLOR, so favorably known to the habitues of the Virginia Springs, and to the visitors at Dagger's last summer.

The surroundings are unusually attractive in point of scenery, with pleasant walks and drives, and the temperature cool and remarkably dry, unequalled perhaps in the latter respect by any place in the Virginia Mountains. Being in the game region of the State, the lovers of sport will find attraction in the deer and bird shooting, trouting in the near streams, and especially Bass fishing in the James River, three miles distant. Large quantities were taken last season.

The waters are a Sulphur and an Iron Spring, upon the grounds, and an Alkaline pool-bath, a short mile from the hotel, to and from which there will be frequent conveyance during bathing hours. The use of this bath is very efficacious in nervous disorders and insomnia, and in affections of the skin.

Of the Sulphur Spring, Doctors WOOD AND KEAN, say "It is adapted to the same class of diseases as the Greenbrier White Sulphur, viz: Chronic affections of the Stomach, Bowels, Liver, Kidneys, Skin, &c., and we believe that invalids would be equally benefitted by a sojourn at this romantic and beautiful place." Some severe cases of neuralgia and rheumatism were effectually cured last season. The great Alum Rock range passes within a few hundred yards of the Hotel.

THE PULASKI ALUM WATERS ALWAYS ON HAND.

ROUND TRIP TICKETS

can be obtained from Baltimore, Washington, Richmond and other points to the Springs, and baggage checked to Clifton Forge, where comfortable stages will meet passengers for the Spring, distant 10 miles, over a good road. Parties arriving either by the morning or evening train will find excellent accommodations at Mr. James D. Ryall's, a half mile from the station, and on the way to the Springs, either for meals, or stopping over night, as they may feel inclined.

We refer by permission to the following gentlemen, late visitors to the Springs:

Gov. WADE HAMPTON, S. C.
Col. C. F. HAMPTON, Mississippi.
THEO. W. NOYES, Washington.
O. BREHME, Baltimore.
J. G. McPHETEERS.
WM. G. WETHERAL,

Gen'l I. R. TRIMBLE,
RICHARD NORRIS, JR.
JOSEPH REYNOLDS,
ROBT. F. BRENT,
DUNCAN C. CLARK,
    and others of Baltimore.

TERMS:

The following low rates of Board have been established: Per day, $2. Per week, $12. Per month, $30 and $35, according to length of time and room accommodations. Children under 10 years of age, and colored nurses half price. Special arrangements for white nurses.

For further particulars, address to the Springs.

BEAN & TAYLOR,
LESSEES.

The Hygeia Hotel, Old Point Comfort, Va.

Situated within 100 yards of Fort Monroe. Open all the year, with ample capacity for 600 guests. Has all modern improvements, elevator, gas and electric bells in every room; water, bath-rooms and closets on each floor. Six daily mails, and telegraph office. Fifteen to twenty first-class steamers land daily, except Sunday, 150 yards from the door. Rooms and halls comfortably heated, and every comfort provided for tourists and health seekers during the Winter. Fire-escapes only fifty feet apart on every floor. Superior beach for bathing at door-steps, and good from May until November. Boating, fishing and driving especially attractive. Send for circular describing hygienic advantages. Terms $2.00 to $3.50 per day, according to locatlon of and number in room, length of stay, etc.

HARRISON PHOEBUS, Proprietor.

What the patrons of The Hygeia Hotel think of it as a place of resort, etc. From the Richmond Dispatch and Petersburg Index-Appeal, July 11th, 1877.

"Visitors to Old Point Comfort. Resolutions Adopted."

"The steamer 'Eliza Honcox' on her trip up the James River, yesterday, brought a large number of ladies and gentlemen, as passengers, on their return home from Old Point Comfort, where they had been the guests of The Hygeia Hotel; among them were Hon. Chas. F. Collier and family, Hon. Robt. H. Jones, Jr., and family, and Mrs. A. W. Archer, of Petersburg; James A. Cowardin, Esq., Thos. H. Norwood, Esq., and family, P. H. Mayo, Esq., and family, T. C. Williams, Esq., and family, Mr. Addison and family, Judge John F. Lay, and Mr. McNeal, of Richmond; and many other influential ladies and gentlemen from other cities. During the passage up James River, a meeting of all the passengers returning from Old Point Comfort, numbering about 100, was held on the steamer 'Hancox.' Mr. James A. Cowardin was called to the chair, and P. H. Mayo was elected secretary, when the following preamble and resolutions, offered by the Hon. Chas. F. Collier of Petersburg, were unanimously adopted.

"WHEREAS, after a short sojourn at that pleasant retreat, Old Point Comfort, it seems meet to testify our appreciation of the great benefits resulting therefrom, and to invite the attention of our Virginia people, as well as those of sister States, to this particular place, as worthy of their most liberal patronage, therefore

"*Resolved*, That this meeting, extemporized on board the steamer 'Eliza Hancox,' appreciating the advantages of Old Point Comfort both as a resort of pleasure and health, do most cordially commend it to the pleasure and health seeking of our own and other communities.

"That we are under a lively sense of the kind care and polite attention of the proprietor, Mr. Phoebus, and his accomplished assistants, and do most confidently assert that nothing was lacking in the accommodations received during our sojourn under his sea-side roof.

"That in connection with our present visit not the least grateful of present impressions is the fact that the Old Point Comfort of to-day is a pleasing picture of the Old Point Comfort of auld lang syne; and that the civilities and courtesies of the officers, both of the army and navy stationed at Fort Monroe, Old Point Comfort and in Hampton Roads, cordially extended and highly appreciated, revived the delightful recollections and tended to restore the happy social relations of days bygone."

Virginia Female Institute,

STAUNTON, VIRGINIA.

INCORPORATED 1844.

RE-ORGANIZED 1865.

VIRGINIA FEMALE INSTITUTE.

INCORPORATED 1844.

Rev. R. H. PHILLIPS, A. M., Rector,

Miss E. FLORENCE PHILLIPS,   -   ·   -   *Principal.*

Miss ANNIE S. PARRAN,   -   -   -   *Vice Principal.*

ASSISTED BY A

FULL CORPS OF EXPERIENCED PROFESSORS AND TEACHERS,

in the Departments of ENGLISH, MATHEMATICS, NATURAL SCIENCES, BELLES-LETTRES, including ENGLISH LITERATURE and HISTORY, MORAL PHILOSOPHY, ANCIENT and MODERN LANGUAGES, INSTRUMENTAL and VOCAL MUSIC, DRAWING & PAINTING, ELOCUTION & PHYSICAL CULTURE.

THE BUILDINGS are heated by steam, lighted with city gas and contain nearly one hundred apartments, affording conveniences rarely equalled.

THE GROUNDS are extensive and afford means for retired, out-door exercise, with shady and dry walks.

THE LOCATION possesses unsurpassed advantages for healthfulness, scenery, pure mountain water and salubrious atmosphere. Railroads, two daily mails and the Telegraph, place it in rapid communication with every part of the country.

The Terms are *uniform* and *lower* than usual in First-Class Schools. It is the object of the Trustees and Directors to offer the *best advantages*, on the lowest terms compatible with this purpose.

SCHOLARSHIPS REDUCE THE TERMS STILL LOWER.

For Catalogues, &c., address Rev. R. H. PHILLIPS, RECTOR, Staunton, Va.

BOARD OF TRUSTEES.

RT. REV. F. M. WHITTLE, D. D., PRESIDENT, Richmond, Va.

REV. CHAS. MINNEGERODE, D. D.	GEO. NEWTON, ESQ.
HON. R. E. WITHERS.	COL. WALTER H. TAYLOR.
GEN. JOSEPH R. ANDERSON.	HON. H. W. SHEFFEY.
MAJ. H. M. BELL.	MAJ. DAVID N. WALKER.
*WM. G. CAZENOVE.	GEN. FRANCIS H. SMITH.
NATHANIEL H. MASSIE.	COL. JAS. H. SKINNER.
JOHN M. MILLER, ESQ.	HON. J N. HENDREN.

* Deceased.

Staunton, Va., April, 1878.

Augusta Female Seminary,

STAUNTON, VA.

MISS MARY J. BALDWIN, Principal.

Largest First-Class School for young ladies in Virginia, and furnished with everything essential to health and comfort.

The Principal is assisted by a large Corps of Experienced and Accomplished Teachers.

Thorough instruction, a high standard of scholarship, refined lady-like deportment, and strict discipline characterize the School. Physical culture amply provided for.

Full Epuivalent Guaranteed for Every Dollar Expended.

School opens

ANNUALLY FIRST WEDNESDAY IN SEPTEMBER,

and closes

CORRESPONDING TIME IN JUNE.

Apply to Principal for Catalogue.

Bath Alum Springs,

BATH CO., VA.,

ten miles from Millboro' depot, Chesapeake and Ohio Railroad.

THE WATERS ARE ALUM AND CHALYBEATE,

and valuable for the cure of

DISPEPSIA, SCROFULA, GENERAL DEBILITY, &C., &C.

The Accommodations are First-class

TERMS:

2.50 per day; 15.00 per week; from 30 to 60 dollars per month,

according to room and time they remain.

For analyses, send for circular.

JOSEPH BAXTER,

Proprietor.

WILLIAM R. TYREE,

DEALER IN

Drugs, Medicines Perfumery,

PAINTS, OILS, VARNISHES, WINDOW GLASS, &C,

NUMBER 6 E. MAIN ST.,

STAUNTON, VIRGINIA.

Physicians' Prescriptions carefully Compounded, and Orders answered with care and dispatch. Farmers and Physicians from the country will find our stock of Medicines complete, warranted genuine, and of the best quality.

STAUNTON FEMALE SEMINARY,

STAUNTON, VIRGINIA.

Rev. J. I. MILLER, A. M., Principal,

—WITH A—

FULL AND EXPERIENCED CORPS OF INSRUCTORS,

—INCLUDING—

Mrs. GENERAL J. E. B. STUART.

TERMS:

For all Expenses, except books, for a Session of forty weeks,

the charge is from $224 to $240.

ADVANTAGES:

Few extras; healthfulness and accessibility of location; thorough and practical instruction; board and home comforts not to be excelled in any school; no sectarian influence allowed, while the greatest interest is manifested in the moral welfare of the pupils; the absence of the many disadvantages of an over crowded school—a GOOD rather than a LARGE school is our aim; economy in dress and general expenditure.

Send to the Principal for Catalogues containing full particulars.

THIS spacious Hotel, the Leading House in the Valley of Virginia, has recently been REFITTED and REPAINTED THROUGHOUT, with

CAPACITY FOR 250 GUESTS!

Located in the central part of the city, ONLY TWO BLOCKS from either Depot.

THE OFFICE IS OPEN THE ENTIRE NIGHT!

And guests will be received or called at any hour.

SPECIAL SUITS OF ROOMS

For Families or Large Traveling Parties.

TOURISTS stopping here can visit in easy distance the celebrated WEYER'S CAVE, and no less famous, the CAVE OF SEVEN FOUNTAINS, both only 15 miles distant over a good road; the wonderful view from "ELLIOTT'S KNOB," and the scenery around the City to be witnessed in an afternoon's drive is the most beautiful in the mountains.

THERE IS A VERY FINE LIVERY ATTACHED TO THE HOTEL,

furnishing Carriages to all points at reasonable rates.

COACHES AND PORTERS IN ATTENDANCE AT ALL THE TRAINS TO CONVEY

Passengers and Baggage Free of Charge.

J. D. CROWLE,
Proprietor.

T. S. DAVIS, Clerk.

AMERICAN HOTEL,

STAUNTON, VA.

A. M. CARTWELL, Proprietor.

This Hotel has changed hands, and is now in COMPLETE ORDER, having been THOROUGHLY RENOVATED AND REFURNISHED, making it the

MOST DESIRABLE HOTEL IN THE VALLEY OF VIRGINIA.

It is near the Chesapeake and Ohio Railroad and the business part of the city, very accessible to all the schools and public institutions of the place.

DELIGHTFULLY COOL IN SUMMER

and commands a beautiful view of the city and surrounding country.

TERMS

ARE REDUCED TO $1.50, $2 and $2.50 PER DAY, ACCORDING TO LOCATION OF ROOMS.

STAUNTON, VIRGINIA,

"The Place,"

THOM. BURKE'S Restaurant and Bar.

Diagonally opposite Virginia Hotel, Staunton, Va.

Good Lodging only 25 cents; Supper, Lodging and Breakfast $1.00. All the delicacies in season served at short notice and LOW RATES.

Bar supplied with the FINEST WHISKEYS, BRANDIES, WINES, CIGARS and TOBACCO.

COOL BERGER AND ENGEL BEER A SPECIALTY.

You will find it to your interest to stop with

THOM. BURKE.

DAVENPORT & MORRIS,
RICHMOND, VA.

IMPORTERS AND WHOLESALE DEALERS IN

SALT,
Agricultural, Liverpool Fine and Ground Alum

SUGARS,
Refined, White and Yellow of all Grades.

COFFEE,
Rio, Laguayra and Java.

TEA,
Gunpowder, Black and English Breakfast.

SYRUP,
Extra Fine and Common.

MOLASSES,
New Orleans and Porto Rico.

BACON,
Sides, Soulders and Hams.

FLOUR,
Family, Extra Superfine and Fine.

FISH,
North Carolina and Eastern Herrings.

POWDER,
Laflin & Rand's Sporting and Blasting.

ALE AND PORTER, English, Scotch and Irish ; Soda, Starch, Soap, Candles, Tobacco, and all leading articles of the Grocery Trade.
Particular attention given to the filling of orders.

65

Jno. M. Keeler,

67

THE
Virginia Mutual Protection Association,

RICHMOND, VA.

Presents a plan by which the

Benfits of Life Insurance may be Secured at Less than Half the Usual Cost.

ORGANIZED FEBRUARY, 1874.

BUSINESS DONE, OVER FIFTEEN MILLION DOLLARS,

PAID TO WIDOWS AND ORPHANS OF DECEASED MEMBERS OVER $150,000.00.

For full information regarding the plan, either call upon, or address the Association.

J. N. WILKINSON, President,

J. W. LOCKWOOD, Auditor,

H. H. WILKINSON, Secretary,

RICHARD IRBY, Vice President,

C. W. P. BROCK, Med. Adviser.

Executive Board.

J. N. WILKINSON, J. THOMPSON BROWN, J. W. LOCKWOOD, JOHN F. ALLEN.

Directors.

J. N. WILKINSON,	President.
JOHN F. ALLEN,	Tobacconist, Franklin Street.
J. D. CRUMP,	Wingo, Ellett & Crump.
H. H. WILKINSON,	Secretary.
J. W. LOCKWOOD,	Cashier National Bank of Va.
RICHARD IRBY,	Supt. Richmond Stove Company.
C. W. P. BROCK, M. D.,	Medical Adviser.
A. B. IRICK,	Prest. Na't B'k, Harrisonburg, Va.
J. THOMPSON BROWN,	Real Estate Agent, 1115 Main St.

68

70

Pure High Grade Fertilizers.

ETIWAN GUANO.

ETIWAN POTASH CHEMICALS

FOR TOBACCO, CORN AND TRUCKING.

ETIWAN DISSOLVED BONE

FOR COMPOSTING.

Etiwan Ash Element.

A first-class Fertilizer for wheat and an excellent top dresser for clover and grass lands. Prepared from formula used so successfully on the poor lands of South Carolina, and by the request and on the recommendation of the Committee on Coast Lands, South Carolina Agricultural Society, a copy of the summary of whose report, published in the Charleston daily papers, will be furnished on application.

ANALYSIS GUARANTEED. WARRANTED PURE.

MANUFACTURED BY

ETIWAN PHOSPHATE COMPANY,

CHARLESTON, S. C.

For circulars and particulars, apply to

Or

WM. A. JAMES,
Gen'l Travelling Agent,
Lock Box 118, Richmond, Va.

WM. C. BEE & CO.,
General Agents,
Adger's Wharf, Charleston, S. C.

FOR SALE BY

W. A. JAMES, Agent,

CORNER 12th & CARY STREETS,

RICHMOND, VA.

74

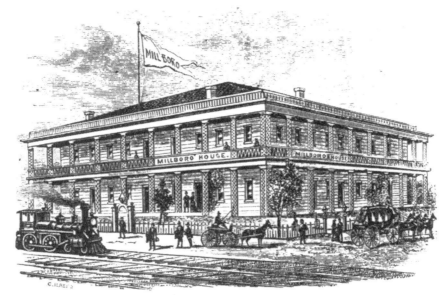

THE ST. JAMES HOTEL,

Pleasantly located at the southeast corner of Capitol Square,

RICHMOND, VA.,

has gained in popular favor and maintained its reputation for uniform cleanliness, first-class fare, prompt and polite attention to guests.

In the centre of the business portion of the city, within one square of the post-office and cu stom-house ; it is, by its retired location, opposite the southeast corner of the beautiful park surrounding the Capitol of Virginia, the most quiet hotel in Richmond.

The proprietor assures the public that he does a bona-fide business, without empty show or senseless exaggeration of advantages.   He simply promises satisfaction and comfort to his guests.

Coaches will attend the arrival of all trains.   Fare 25 cents.   To and from steamers 50 cents.

T. W. HOENNIGER, Proprietor.

Charges reduced to $2.50 and $2 per day, according to size and location of room—with uniformity in every other respect.   Board at reasonable rates.

Salmon, Hancock & Co.,

FACTORY 35, RICHMOND, VA.

Awarded highest medal for

PLUG AND TWIST TOBACCO.

WE MANUFACTURE

THE BEST TOBACCO

in the world.

Manufacturers and Owners

of the

Celebrated Brands

FOUR SEASONS,
WHITE MOUNTAIN,
GOLDEN NUGGET,
OUT OF THE SEA,
OPERA,
DWARF ROSES,
MARITANA,
ZULEIKA,
LITTLE GIANT,

MERRIMAC,
RUSTIC,
"OUR GUIDE,"
SOVEREIGN OVER ALL,
BELL'S LIFE,
MANIE,
SUNSHINE,
BESSIE STANFORD,
GOLDEN AGE,

ATLANTIC CABLE TWIST,
MAY QUEEN TWIST,
BIG LICK NAVY POUNDS,
VIRGINIA JOYS,
SUCCESS,
MAY FLOWER TWIST,
SOMETHING NEW,
OUR PET POUNDS,
STANDARD STATE POUNDS,

Trade mark—"IT SHINES FOR ALL."

78

METROPOLITAN WORKS,

CANAL STREET FROM SIXTH TO SEVENTH,
RICHMOND, VIRGINIA.

ENGINES, PORTABLE AND STATIONARY;

SAW-MILLS, GRIST-MILLS, BOILERS, CASTINGS OF BRASS AND IRON, FORGINGS, &c., MACHINERY FOR GOLD AND COAL MINES, BLAST FURNACES, &c.

We call special attention to our IMPROVED PORTABLE ENGINES for agricultural purposes. Also, to our new styles SMALL LOCOMOTIVES *for hauling lumber* and other articles upon tramways and narrow-gauge railways. Our strictly portable ENGINE for THRASHING, GINNING, &c., is pronounced by the most intelligent planters the best in use. Also manufacturers of Pulleys, Shafting, and Hangers. Jones' Patent Tobacco Lump Machine to work by hand or power.

SEND FOR ILLUSTRATED CATALOGUE, which will be furnished free.

WM. E. TANNER & CO.

IF YOU WANT TO GO ANYWHERE.

East, West, North or South,

ASK FOR TICKETS VIA

CHESAPEAKE AND OHIO RAILWAY.

MECHUM'S RIVER HOUSE,

Is immediately on the Chesapeake and Ohio Railroad, about 200 yards from the Depot and Postoffice, 10 miles from the University of Virginia, 170 from Richmond; the House is

LARGE, AIRY, NEATLY & COMFORTABLY FURNISHED.

LARGE AND SHADY YARD.

Chalybeate Water on the Premises.

WE MAKE OUR TERMS TO SUIT THE TIMES.

C. H. PRICE,

Mechum's River, Albemarle Co., Va.

80

THE
Chesapeake & Ohio Railway,

THE ROUTE FOR THE TOURIST,

Presenting more beautiful views and magnificent scenery than any other in the world.

THE ROUTE FOR THE INVALID,

Possessing the best means for ease and comfort in transportation; dry, pure air, healthy locations for rest, and the greatest variety of mineral waters, on and near its line.

THE ROUTE FOR THE PLEASURE-SEEKER,

Exhibiting the most wonderful views and marvels of Nature and leading to Famous Resorts, various in kind and degree, from those for the gay and fashionable, where the votaries of pleasure know no rest, to the quiet summer home in the cool and breezy mountain shades.

THE ROUTE FOR BUSINESS MEN,

Being the shortest line between the Atlantic Seaboard and the great Valleys of the Ohio and Mississippi Rivers, passing the mountain barriers with the gentlest curves and easiest grades of any East and West line in the United States.

THE ROUTE FOR THE SPORTSMAN AND ANGLER,

To the best *hunting* and *fishing* grounds of *Virginia* and *West Virginia*, including in their variety of *game* and *fish*, deer, bear, wild turkeys, wild ducks, grouse, quail, snipe, woodcock, mountain trout, bass, pike, pickerel, &c., &c.

THE ROUTE FOR ALL PERSONS

Whose *business* or *pleasure* requires transportation East or West.

THE ONLY ROUTE TO THE FAMOUS MINERAL SPRINGS,

And Mountain Resorts of the Blue Ridge and Alleghanies of the Virginias.

81

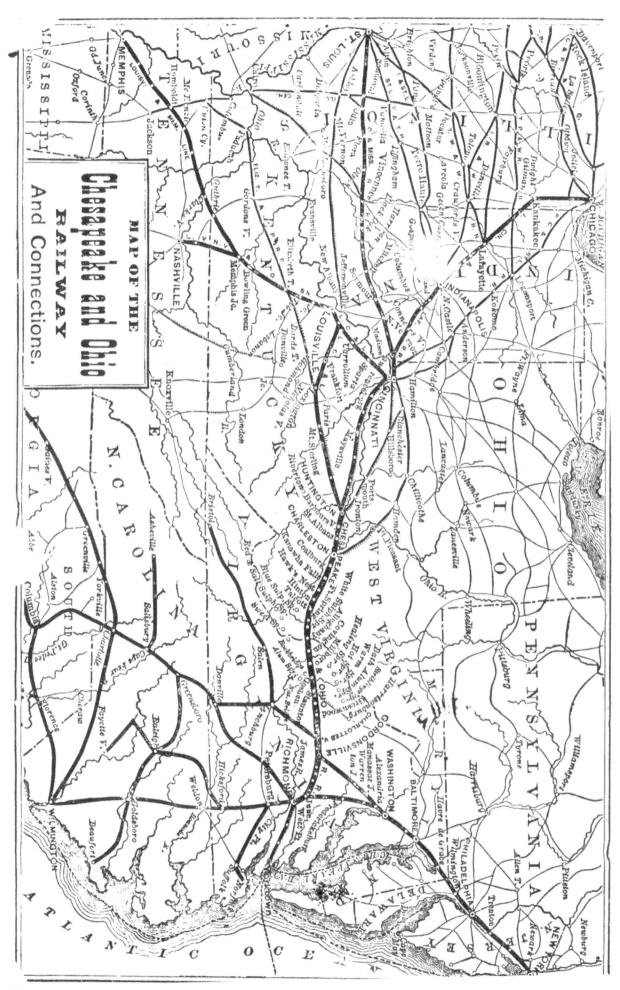

MAP OF THE
Chesapeake and Ohio
RAILWAY
And Connections.

82

Made in the USA
Monee, IL
23 June 2023